James Dixon's Children

by
Melanie Warren

with assistance from James Dixon's own writings

Published by GAZELLE BOOKS
White Cross Mills, Hightown, Lancaster LA1 4XS

A catalogue record for this book is available from the British Library.

ISBN: 1855860171
EAN: 9781855860179

Printed by Book Printing UK
Remus House, Coltsfoot Drive, Peterborough, PE2 9BF

Acknowledgements

We acknowledge the generations of managers and staff who kept safe and secure the archives of Blackburn Orphanage, as well as those involved most recently in the huge task of digitising and archiving this treasure trove of documents.

An invaluable source for the present work was *The Blackburn Samaritan* by Trevor Moore, 1990, Landy Publishing. Much credit is due to the late Mr Moore's diligent research, in particular for his histories of both James Dixon's and Jane McLellan's families. We thank Trevor's widow for her permission to use this research and the original history produced by her husband.

The author would also like to thank the following individuals and organisations who helped to produce this book:

the Heritage Lottery Fund for providing a grant for the original archives project in 2011 and without which this book might never have been produced.

the Trustees of Child Action Northwest for permission to pursue this project and John Tempest for allowing full access to the orphanage's archives.

Nancy Hill and the family of James Dixon for their encouragement and the loan of James Dixon's personal diary as well as the donation of Jane Dixon's recipe book.

David Tilsley and the Lancashire County Record Office for advising on the preservation of documents and helping to develop an archival indexing system.

archiving volunteers including Trish Keelan-Smalley, Lynne Bell and John Bailey.

Diana Rushton of Blackburn Library and the Local History Department for her research assistance.

Mike Johnson for providing the necessary equipment to digitally preserve the orphanage's Admission Books, and his photographic record of the work so far achieved by the grant from the Heritage Lottery Fund.

Harriet Roberts, Creative Partnerships Manager at Child Action Northwest, for giving the author the opportunity to explore this fascinating aspect of Blackburn's history and to compile this book.

Gordon Fairweather, Bernard Kennedy, Martin Cottam, Barbara Riding, Sue Cotton, Ian Holmes and also Ray Smith, from the Blackburn Local History Society.

Peggy Holmes, Lesley Marklew, Andrew Kay and Linda Wilkinson for their painstaking proofreading.

Thanks are especially due to Toby Hargreaves for his cover image. The challenge of designing the cover of this book was taken on by Blackburn College, who gave the project to their Foundation Art and Design students. The project, which resulted in a competition between five students, allowed them to visit the archive room at the old orphanage in Wilpshire for inspiration, where they viewed old documents belonging to James, such as his diary and personal photos. The final book cover ideas were then pitched to the author, Melanie Warren, and a judging panel.

The eventual winner was nineteen year old Toby Hargreaves, who then revealed that he had been fostered by his grandparents at the age of eleven. He used his experiences of being a foster child to influence his design for the cover of this book.

Toby, who designed a three-dimensional model of butterflies flying out of the orphanage building, said, 'I know how the fostering process works and how it can sometimes make you feel trapped by your past. I have learnt to not let things get me down and, like the orphans, I have grown up, moved on and made a life for myself. The butterflies represent the freedom that both I and the orphans have shared.'

Joanne Conlon, lecturer at Blackburn College, said, 'This was a project very close to Toby's heart and he did a fantastic job of encapsulating his personal feelings, which are shared by many others in his position. All the students involved stepped up to the mark and produced some great work for such a worthy project.'

Harriet Roberts, Creative Partnerships Manager at Child Action Northwest, said, 'We were really impressed with the students' commitment and creative ideas. The final cover is of the highest quality and illustrates the excellent standards of the students and the College.'

Finally, the author would like to thank James Dixon, for his intelligent and insightful writings in all their forms. This book has been compiled from a variety of sources including contemporary documents but extensive use has been made of James Dixon's own writings. Such excerpts appear in italics and no attempt has been made to update the language to make it more palatable to modern tastes. The author makes no apology for this, as she believes that James's original voice deserves to be heard.

Foreword

By Nancy Hill, granddaughter of James Dixon.

When I was a little girl I could never understand why people were surprised when I said that my mother was born in an orphanage. But she and her two sisters had a very happy childhood there, playing with the other children and waiting their turn for a ride on Ponto, the Orphanage donkey.

I always knew there were many Orphanage papers safely stored in the cellars, but I did not realise what an excellent administrator James Dixon was, understanding the importance of keeping a careful record of each child from the very first day of their arrival.

Now, this substantial archive has been scanned and catalogued and Melanie has been able to make good use of the detailed records to write this fascinating account, not only of James Dixon's life and work, but also of the development of the Orphanage and the lives of the children who lived there.

When the children reached school leaving age at fourteen, he was most careful to find a suitable work placement for each one and those who could continue their education did so – my mother and her sister went to Accrington Technical College with them and she described how they ran along the road to Wilpshire Station to catch the train each morning.

Every child needs the individual care and attention which James Dixon did his best to provide for every one of the Orphanage children and it is deeply satisfying to know that this work still continues at the Orphanage building, although in a very different form more suitable for the continuing needs of the children of today.

Thank you, Melanie, for a wonderful book.

CHAPTER ONE

James Dixon, born in Annan, Scotland in 1855, was the founder of Blackburn Orphanage and was, during his lifetime, a well-known Blackburn personality and charity worker. His philanthropy was not unusual; in Victorian times many wealthy men and women used their riches for good works. James Dixon, however, was not a wealthy man and this makes his achievements so much more remarkable. By trade he was a joiner, apprenticed to his father's business at sixteen. As a young man he was a dedicated Sunday School teacher, so when his apprenticeship finished and he moved to work in Carlisle, he at once sought out a church where he could continue this unpaid teaching role. At twenty-two he moved to Blackburn, volunteered as a Sunday School teacher and soon became very concerned at the level of poverty amongst his young pupils. Three years later, he and his friend John Thomas Walkden set out to raise enough money to open a Ragged School in a disused and run down plumber's shop. This was followed by two small residential homes for boys and girls and, finally, a full-scale orphanage in Wilpshire, near Blackburn.

Amongst the remarkably extensive archives of the Blackburn Orphanage, there is one piece of paper on which is written a kind of wish list, compiled by James towards the end of his life. It set out what his youthful dreams had been and which of them he had managed to realise.

1. *To purchase the whole 100 acres of Tipping's Farm and 50 acres of Hollies Farm and so control future buildings on the land.*
   Result – Only 5 acres of Tipping's was bought and none of Hollies Farm.

2. *To have two Homes built, one for boys & one for girls.*
   Result – These have now been built.

3. *To build a sanatorium.*
   Result – Not built.

4. *To have a holiday home for boys at St. Anne's on Sea.*
   Result – Not done.

5. *To have a holiday home for girls at Southport.*
   Result – Not done.

6. *To raise an Endowment Fund of £100,000.*
   Result – £50,000 raised.

7. *To have a working boys home in Town.*
   Result – Not done.

Considering how much this one man did manage to accomplish, reading his list of unattained goals is disheartening, as if he reached his old age feeling that there was much more he could have done. Yet, what he did achieve is a lengthy catalogue of success. Since James began his mission to help needy children, around four thousand children have found a safe place and the chance of a new life through the intercession of the organisations brought into being by his enthusiasm and determination. Surely no one could argue that this was not a life well-lived.

James Dixon died in 1936, but his mission to help needy children did not end there. The work James started over a century ago continues today. The original Boys' Orphanage building no longer survives, but the Girls' Orphanage building still stands. It is home now to Child Action Northwest, a charity which continues James's work with disadvantaged children and young people in Lancashire and further afield.

In the voluminous cellars of this century-old building, a hundred years' worth of records, ledgers, files, plans and other paperwork resided untouched. In 2010, a team of volunteers was recruited and given the task of cataloguing these books and papers, and a ground floor room in the building was transformed into a dedicated Archive Room. It soon became clear that, in terms of historical importance, the dusty papers and ledgers comprised a collection described by Lancashire Records Office as 'unique' in its completeness. It seems that we have James Dixon himself to thank for this. Examination of the collection proves him to be an inveterate record keeper, with a penchant for filing systems. He had a sense of the importance of preserving even the smallest notes on scraps of paper and the backs of envelopes, if they were relevant to a child's history.

For every child admitted to the orphanage there was an Admission Form, containing information about the child's family and circumstances. Along with this a Medical Form was completed either by the child's family doctor or, quite often, by Dr Pollard who was on the board of trustees and who gave his services to the orphanage at no cost. All the information on these forms was then transcribed by James into the Admission Books and the original forms filed and carefully cross referenced. James also regularly wrote in the Occurrences Book, in which he recorded daily happenings in the orphanage, reports on visits and inspections by officials, staff holidays, children's days out to the seaside, and more.

In addition to these books and documents, the orphanage's archives contain numerous photographs of children and staff, James Dixon's family and that of his wife, Jane McLellan.

All of this treasure would have been more than enough raw material to fashion a book about James Dixon and his work, but for a long time one vital piece was known to be missing. In a short biography written in the 1970s, the author included various passages from James Dixon's Diary. It became apparent that this diary was not his Occurrences Book. It was assumed that there was a personal diary – but it could not be found. The cellar was searched on several occasions but the elusive diary failed to surface.

A year after work on the archives began, a lady from Leeds called Nancy Hill was visiting old haunts in Clitheroe. For old times' sake she bought a copy of the Clitheroe Advertiser. As luck would have it, this edition carried a piece about the fund-raising efforts of Child Action Northwest and, more specifically, an Orphanage Open Day, which would be happening later that month. Nancy contacted the organisers and attended the Open Day as a guest of honour – because James Dixon just happened to be her grandfather! Nancy had in her possession a number of treasures connected with James and the orphanage; letters, papers and the elusive James Dixon's personal diary.

The diary was the final piece in the puzzle, and an invaluable piece, as it allows us to discover James Dixon as a young man. It helps us to understand the early experiences that resulted in the drive and determination of the man, whose achievements were the result of a moral imperative so strong it brooked no argument. It helps us to answer the question: 'Who was James Dixon?'

CHAPTER TWO

James Dixon's diary is a single notebook, hardbacked, with hardly a blank space on its two hundred pages. In fact, the notebook belonged first to James Dixon's father, (also James) who used it to record a number of essays of his own devising. These essays were all written in the early 1840s, in a relatively short space of time, completed well before James senior was thirty. It may have been the only time in his life James senior attempted to be a writer. If he did write anything else, it has not yet been discovered.

James senior's handwriting is a small and meticulous copperplate. Whilst the essays have no great literary merit, they are well written and the subjects are decidedly Christian in tone: health, clean living and temperance. They bear titles such as *'To Produce Agreeableness'* and *'Liberty of Consciences'*. The structure of these essays is good; clearly the subjects were dear to the heart and James senior had spent a great deal of time ruminating and considering before committing his thoughts to paper.

There were only a handful of essays, so most of the notebook was blank when James senior gave it to his son, James, who used it to record not only a diary but also quotations from poets, philosophers and Bible commentaries. He also recorded lists of facts and figures, his accounts, tips for home remedies and even jokes. The first dated entry is in November 1877, when he was just twenty-two, and the last, a note of the passing of a family member, is dated July 17th 1933. Only three years later, James himself passed away, aged eighty.

Little could his father have known, when entrusting that little book of essays to his twenty-two year old son, that he would keep that notebook close and put it to good use for the next fifty-six years of his life.

James Dixon senior's writings are clearly illustrative of his character and his morals; both the essays and the man must have influenced his son's own character. The first essay in the book deals with his attitude to the evils of drink. The essay is dated January 2nd 1844, bears the title *The Dram Shop* and describes an incident which happened to James senior on the previous night. He came across four whisky sozzled and high spirited men having a loud conversation in the street. No allowance was made for the fact that it was New Year's Day. What James senior saw and heard appalled him.

Last night a circumstance came under my observation which produced a large amount of sensation. As I had occasion to pass by one of those places called Dram Shops - or to give them a name approaching nearer to their professions - one of those places where fools get dressed and prepared to serve in public life. Four bipeds were just removing from this noted university, no doubt after each had received a degree or more of the professor's heterogenous composition. And thinking that I might receive some information from the circumstance, as from everything in existence some good is derivable, therefore accommodated myself the scene by walking within hearing and seeing of the four collegians. It was one of the most disgustful figures of human wretchedness and misery the eye could witness.

As James senior eavesdropped, it transpired that their conversation was all about drink – specifically, the quality of the whisky they had just consumed in the Dram Shop and the mysteries of the delicate process of distillation. One of their number was explaining the process to the others who were novices to the art, despite the fact that Annan itself was home to a distillery which had been built ten years previously. One can imagine that James senior had witnessed detrimental changes in the town and its people since the distillery arrived, and that these changes must have dismayed him.

Amongst the numerous vicious habits & customs which infest society, unquestionably intoxication stands as one of the most prominent. It gives license to every sort of vice – protects in a measure all abuses – creates the most malevolent motives – originates the most contentious combinations – destroys the most elevated society together; and in the end, leads to the most disastrous consequences. Certainly this calls for sympathy, which is in existence, to come forward and aid in order that this most abominable, most useless, most detestable, soul and body destroying practice may be annihilated.

It is interesting that the last sentence calls for sympathy; alcohol is seen as the evil-doer and those who have fallen foul of its charms should be helped, somehow, to rid themselves of its influence over them. Another of James senior's essays, *'To Produce Agreeableness'*, explains that in order to make others respect us, *'we should endeavour to make ourselves always well pleased with every person we have any thing to do; and appear to be more entertained than desirous of giving entertainment.'*

A third essay, which takes up several pages, is entitled *'Liberty of Consciences'* and discusses the lack of moral fibre preventing some people from taking *'correct action'*. There are circumstances pushing from one side for the thing to be done – and there are circumstances pushing from the other side for the thing not to be done. Which is stronger? He suggests, rather controversially, that there are certain classes of society who have not had the opportunity to develop their minds sufficiently to enable them to take decisions instead of allowing circumstances to dictate their actions.

These essays were written more than a decade before James Junior was born. They were written when James senior was himself a young man in his twenties. For his son, reading these essays when he was the same age must have been enlightening. Few people have the opportunity to learn first-hand from diaries, letters or, indeed, essays, how their parents felt and thought as young people. The essays show that James senior held strong opinions even as a young man and there is every reason to believe that he held these opinions for the rest of his life. It is easy to assume that James junior must have been influenced by his father's strong personality, his deeply moral character and his Christian belief.

Certainly, as we learn more about James junior's life, echoes of these essays can be found in the way he conducted himself and doggedly pursued his ambitions. He encouraged abstinence from alcohol in all the children and young people he took under his wing, he earned the greatest respect from everyone with whom he came into contact, and never could he be accused of allowing circumstances to prevent him from taking the correct action as dictated by his conscience.

James Dixon senior was a man worthy of respect. His own father, John, had been a farmer, with more than two hundred acres under his care, but James decided to train as a joiner, and by the time he was thirty-five had his own business, employing three men. He married Isabella Imrie in 1842 and they moved to Liverpool, where they would remain for nine years, near to Isabella's family. Records do not show any children born in those first nine years – only after moving back to Annan were their three boys born: John in 1852, James in 1855, and Benjamin in 1859.

The family joinery business grew until James was employing six men. James junior's childhood was not luxurious and the family home was of a modest size. However, James senior was respected in the town. By the neatness of the handwriting in his essays, we can deduce that he was educated and that he was intelligent, thoughtful, and a man of strong opinions and Christian morals. He ran a business and must have had some ability with finances, because he was eventually elected as Annan's Borough Treasurer, a role he fulfilled for some years. More notably, he is also remembered for being, along with other members of Annan's town council, one of Annan's 'Seven Wise Men': the committee which forwarded the idea that a viaduct should be built across the Solway Firth.

The viaduct would carry a railway and would connect Annan and Bowness-on-Solway. Its main purpose would be to carry iron ore from Cumberland to Scotland much faster than by road, which would bring more prosperity to Annan and the surrounding area. It was a radical idea and a tremendous feat of engineering, as it would have to be over a mile long.

The viaduct took over three years to build and was opened to passengers in 1870. It carried traffic for the next forty years, until changes in trade and overseas imports led to the viaduct falling gradually into disuse. It finally closed entirely in 1921 – although the residents of Annan and other nearby villages continued to use it as a footbridge, particularly on Sundays, when alcohol could not be bought in their own country. It is recorded that as the viaduct began to crumble from disuse, a gate and a guard had to be installed, after one or two 'happy' residents lost their lives on the precarious journey home.

James Dixon senior was not personally involved in the engineering or the building of the viaduct but he and the other 'Wise Men' were officially invited to the foundation ceremony, the Cutting of the First Sod. The event was commemorated in a poem, written by Provost (Mayor) Palmer and published on March 28th 1865. It began:

In Annan there were seven wise men
That laid their heads together;
'What can be done for our good old town?'
They speared at ane anither.
'What can be done for this Ancient Burgh –
A good old Burgh is she –
Oh! could we but some scheme devise
To bring prosperity.'

The poem, which runs to twenty-four verses, mentions each of the 'Wise Men' in turn and their names were listed below it; *Mr Alex Downie, Town Clerk; Mr Bailie Kerr, Builder; Mr Cuthbertson, Publisher; Mr Jackson, Brickmaker; Mr John Cunningham, Ironmonger; Mr Jas. Dixon, Borough Treasurer; Mr Carruthers, Surveyor.* Each man is referred to obliquely in the poem, so that James Dixon is referred to thus:

The man that smooths the timber board,
And keeps the Burgh's purse...

To be immortalised in a poem is quite an honour, no matter who the author and what the occasion. Many copies of the poem were printed on high quality, weighty paper, to be distributed amongst those present at the ceremony and at least one copy still exists, in James Dixon's papers now in the possession of his granddaughter, Nancy Hill.

To return to the diary... as well as essays by James senior, the notebook also contains some by James junior, although they appear more like school essays than personal attempts at literary expression. One notable example, entitled '*Man*', is basically a list of facts about the human body and mankind in general, from the number of bones in the human body and the number of pores in a square inch of skin, to the average weight and height of different nationalities. The list includes some shocking facts: '*the average duration of life in towns is 38 years, in the country 55 years. 150 children out of 1,000 die during the first year of their birth; 50 more during the 2nd year; 58 more during the next three years; and 19 more during the next two years. Thus 277 die in 7 years from their birth.*'

These thought-provoking statistics were not wasted on James. On a different page James recorded this quotation: '*delicate threads of life may snap at any moment*'.

Another essay, on '*Health*', deals in detail with all the needs of a healthy body: food, warmth, cleanliness, exercise, fresh air, rest, and light. Full of good sense, it runs to nine or ten pages. Its lessons were thoroughly learned and put into practice by James, throughout his own life and in all his later work with disadvantaged children.

One page in the notebook is headed '*Things Not Generally Known by British Youth*' and is signed and dated; '*J. Dixon Junior, Carlisle, 13 June 1877*'. It contains many quotes about the evils and the pernicious nature of tobacco, for even then, learned men were commenting that tobacco was harmful. James quotes Dr Fergus Fergusson as saying, '*I believe that no one who smokes tobacco before the bodily powers are developed ever makes a strong, vigorous man* and Dr H Gibbons pronounced that *Tobacco impairs digestion, poisons the blood, depresses the vital powers, causes the limbs to tremble and weakens and otherwise disorders the heart.'* Some quotes are from unnamed sources, but are as true today as they were then: *'The use of tobacco is one of the most powerful accessories of the temptations to drinking which surround British youths.'* Another quote states its case a little more poetically, *'Smoking is one of the legs upon which drunkenness rests.'*

James used other pages in the notebook to record his wages and outgoings, favourite stanzas from poets he admired, such as Byron, and notes from Bible commentaries. One of his diary notes mentions that he had collected a Bible commentary from a friend, Dr Grosart, and a whole page in the notebook is filled with lines which clearly come from such a book. Research has found that the quotations are from a six-volume *Complete Commentary of the Bible*, written in 1706 by Matthew Henry. The book provides an exhaustive look at every single verse in the Bible and must have taken James some time to examine, but examine it he did, noting down lines which resonated with him:

You may apprehend but cannot comprehend...
All our knowledge must be in order to practice...
Men may be truly devout though they do not abound in the expressions of devotion...
Those persons or actions we can say no good of we had best say nothing of...
Most of the meats forbidden as unclean were also unwholesome...
Saul lost his kingdom for want of 2 or 3 hours patience...
You may as soon find a living man without breath as a living Christian without prayer...
Hard arguments do best with soft words...
Hard words indeed break no bones but many a heart has been broken by them...
First or last sinners must be weepers...
War is a tragedy which destroys the stage upon which it is acted...

There was also one quotation on this page from Francis Bacon, the 16th century English philosopher and statesman, *'Money is like muck; good for nothing if it is not spread.'* This pithy statement may well have informed James's later attitude to money: that those with much money should be encouraged to give for the benefit of the deserving poor.

Although James clearly had a very serious and studious side to his nature, he also had a sense of humour. He even jotted down occasional jokes in his notebook. *'The Quaker sold the horse saying that it had only two faults – he would tell one before it was sold (that it was bad to catch) and one after the purchase (that it was no use when it was catched).'* And this quip is as relevant now as it was then, *'The little girl was asked where liars went to – to New York to write newspapers.'*

James's notebook also records notes made for his Sunday School lessons and addresses, for he was an ardent Sunday School teacher. He taught at the United Presbyterian Church in Annan, the church now known as St Andrew's, but soon proved himself to be more than just a teacher. He took his role seriously and involved himself in the organisation of the school, proposing in April of 1877 that prizes should be given for attendance – a suggestion that was agreed upon.

James had joined his father's joinery business as an apprentice in 1871, when he was sixteen years old. His apprenticeship was completed in 1877, when he was twenty-one. James then started to apply for jobs elsewhere; he applied to a builder in Aspatria for the position of Builder's Clerk and applied for a similar situation in Liverpool. However, for the time being he continued to work with his father. The two of them moved temporarily to Carlisle, to work on a contract for the construction of three houses in the town. This move meant that James had to leave his Sunday School scholars behind. A diary entry on April 29th records; *'I was today presented with a handsome book by the scholars in my class at the Sunday School bearing the following inscription 'presented to James Dixon by his Sunday School Scholars on the occasion of his leaving Annan, as a mark of regard for his services during his stay with them.''*

In fact he didn't actually move permanently for another month, but worked in Carlisle during the week and came home at weekends, continuing to visit the Sunday School. This gave him time to organise a special treat for his scholars. On May 12th he took five excited boys from his class to have a group photograph taken at W. Irvine's Photographers. He ordered twelve prints at a cost of seven shillings. When the prints arrived a fortnight later, he sent copies to each of his ex-scholars, and noted in his diary the many *nice letters* he received in return. He would continue to keep in touch with his students, but he would never return to live in his home town permanently.

On May 22nd 1877, James moved to Carlisle for good. Once he had settled into his new lodgings, he immediately sought out the nearest United Presbyterian church and introduced himself as an experienced Sunday School teacher. He was accepted at once, and the following weekend was given a class of scholars. The next Sunday, he was disconcerted to find that he had a different group of children to teach and he complained about it in his diary. To be presented with yet another group of children the following week was too much and the earnest young man made his feelings known. Finally, at the end of July, this determined twenty-one year old was given a proper, permanent class of eight scholars. He was voted in as a permanent teacher on August 6th.

James's diary clearly shows how very active he was and what an enquiring nature he possessed. Moving to Carlisle in May, he spent what remained of the year attending meetings of the Band of Hope (a temperance organisation for boys) at various churches, as well as attending Anniversary meetings at the Methodist, Wesleyan and Primitive Sunday Schools. He lists the following *'interesting meetings'*: The Young Man's Mutual Improvement Society, Carlisle Debating Club, Religious Debating Class, Vestry Meetings, Political and Temperance Meetings and Templar Soirees. He also attended Bible classes and in his spare time he sometimes sat in on court hearings, acquainting himself with their procedures.

He frequently went home to Annan at weekends, visited relatives there and in the surrounding villages and on Sundays attended his old Sunday School, often teaching his old students again. In October 1877 he records that three of his old scholars, along with some of his relatives, came on a special visit to Carlisle, to witness a royal visit to the town. He continued to be actively concerned with his old scholars' welfare and spent time talking with them. He listened attentively and took them seriously. When he learned, for example, that they were not satisfied with their new teacher, he spoke to the minister about it and gained assurances that things would change.

It is clear that James was not a man to waste his time or his energy. In case we were in any doubt, his diary entries for late December emphasise his desire to use his time usefully and not waste a minute in idleness. One evening in late December, he and two friends went along to the local School of Art and signed up for a class in mechanical drawing, to start in January. The following night he attended a lecture on Livingstone. Three evenings later (his twenty-second birthday) he was at a lecture on the Ten Lost Tribes. The following evening he attended Bible Class and the evening after that a lecture on the Pyramids of Egypt. Even on Christmas Day, he busied himself in making a T-square and a drawing board for his up-coming course at the School of Arts and on Boxing Day he travelled home to Annan to attend meetings of Annan's Debating Club and the Band of Hope.

The Band of Hope was an organisation close to James's heart. It was a temperance organisation aimed specifically at poor working class children, who were required to take a pledge of abstinence from alcohol but were rewarded with a variety of enjoyable activities and days out to the seaside in the summer months. James sought out the Carlisle branch of the Band of Hope and attended regularly. He continued to support the movement throughout his life, adopting its tenets for use in his own dealings with children and young people.

At his new Sunday School in Carlisle, James involved himself wholeheartedly, as he had done in Annan, doing far more than simply teaching Bible stories, but working also to contribute to the organisation and management of the school. In January 1878, he took the slightly risky decision to engage his scholars in drawing up their own rules for the management of their class. This clever use of reverse psychology, combined with several weeks' work on the part of the scholars, resulted in a set of twelve sensible, firm rules. These were then submitted to the school's Superintendent, who considered them and gave them his approval. The class then voted to adopt their own rules which, of course, they did unanimously. This is an interesting example of James's understanding of, and respect for, children and their feelings.

In March 1878 James enrolled at the School of Art for two more courses: geometry and perspective drawing. As usual he took his self-education very seriously. When the school was closed for its regular week's holiday, he and two friends obtained the key from their master and went to school by themselves on three occasions during the week. Naturally, he passed all three courses.

In May, James recorded in his diary that his Sunday School had given an evening *'entertainment'*, where two of his own scholars had *'recited pieces'*. There was also a spelling bee and two of his scholars won prizes. The meeting was also an opportunity for general prize-giving; seven of his scholars won prizes for their good attendance. It is not surprising, then, to hear how dismayed these children were to learn, a couple of months later, that James was moving on again and leaving Carlisle. Their last Sunday lesson with James was on July 14th. James's young scholars suggested that they abandon class for the day, to which James agreed. They all invited him to visit them in their homes, to which he also agreed. He visited them the following evening and noted in his diary that he was *'sorry to part with them'*.

James Dixon arrived in Blackburn on July 18th 1878, at 4.30 in the afternoon. He was twenty-two years old, and he would stay in Blackburn for the rest of his life.

CHAPTER THREE

James Dixon's reasons for choosing Blackburn as a destination are simple – he was looking for work. On arriving, he immediately went out to hunt for a job. He was fortunate to find one at once, to start the following Monday with local joinery company, Messrs Marshall and Dent. On the Sunday, he (naturally) attended a nearby church and Sunday School. A few days later he wrote to all his Carlisle scholars to let them know how he was getting along and, no doubt, to encourage them to behave themselves and attend to their lessons. Several of them wrote back and stayed in touch for at least a few months.

During his brief stay in Carlisle, James had set out to systematically visit every church he could find. He kept a list, which shows us that between November 1877 and May 1878 he had visited an astonishing seventeen different churches of all denominations. When he moved to Blackburn, he continued in the same way, visiting ten different churches in his first six months and at least six more in the following year. James may have been searching for a church in which he felt comfortable and to whose congregation he felt he could belong. But his dedication to the hunt shows something else in the man – a questioning spirit and openness to religious denominations different from his own. However, as James was Presbyterian there was little doubt that St George's Church on Mount Street would become his regular church and, within a month of arriving in Blackburn, he was invited to act as a Sunday School teacher there. It was here that he met the aforementioned Rev Dr Grosart, who played such a major part in his continuing religious education, lent him a Bible commentary and, indeed, would later preside at his marriage.

James must have felt at home in Blackburn, for within six months he was considering bringing his parents, who were advancing in years, to live with him there. This idea had to be shelved for a while, however, as early in 1879 employment was suddenly in short supply. Any available work was poorly paid, with the pay rate for joiners and other tradespeople being severely reduced. James was forced to hunt for work in other towns, especially Preston, but without any luck.

His work at the Sunday School progressed regardless and no doubt benefitted from the fact that he was out of work and had time on his hands. As there was no Band of Hope in Blackburn, James suggested that one should be set up and was promptly appointed Secretary of a committee to do just that. But although he managed to fill his time usefully, he recorded in his diary that he was longing for a letter from home, as he was *'very low-spirited'*. He had been out of work for a fortnight and his prospects of finding any employment seemed *'black'*. He wrote home himself, enclosing a paper he had written about his planned Band of Hope. He received a reply a couple of days later, which must have cheered him. He ventured to Preston searching for work on at least two more occasions, without success, and then, having now been out of work for over a month, James decided to go home for a holiday. His diary says, *'Went home to Annan today, meeting with mother gladdened my heart and cheered my soul.'* He stayed in Annan for almost a whole month, continuing to apply for jobs from a distance.

It was April 15th before James returned to Blackburn, having finally found a short-term job with a building company. The job lasted just a month, by which time tradesmen's wages had fallen yet again, from 8½d to 7½d an hour. He then suffered another two months of unemployment, before taking a job in July with Marshall & Dent of Limbrick, the first company he had worked with in Blackburn. His father had kept him going financially by sending small amounts of cash by postal order. Of course his time out of work was not wasted; he simply devoted more of his time to his Sunday School students. The newly established Band of Hope was launched in May 1879, with over thirty children attending – a number which would grow. June saw a Sunday School trip to Morecambe, which began when the whole class and teachers met at the school door at 4.30 in the morning! The day out was packed, with high-spirited boys enjoying rides, the beach and the swimming baths. It was midnight before they arrived back in

Blackburn. Happily, James was also able to spend a little time during the day with his father, who happened to be working in nearby Carnforth.

James also continued his education during 1879, with courses and examinations in building construction, geometry, mathematics and, oddly, animal physiology. In October, his job now more secure, he revived the idea of bringing his mother to live with him in Blackburn and received 'a grand letter' from her, expressing her willingness to do so. James found a suitable house for them to share at 23 Blackburn Street and she moved to Blackburn in mid-November.

Now James had a proper house which was more like a home than his previous rented rooms. He was able, on occasion, to entertain. Just two months after moving in, in January 1880, he hosted a tea party for twenty of his Sunday School scholars. 'Tea commenced at 6.30 pm, after tea a long programme of songs, recitations, music brought a very pleasant evening to a close at 10 pm, all being vastly pleased.'

Also in that month he was appointed to be his church's representative at the Sunday School Conference which would be held in Bury on Good Friday. He was required to give a report of the conference to the teachers' meeting at St George's, after the event. This was his first experience of such responsibility and it would not be his last.

Now aged twenty-four, and encouraged by the trust and responsibility given to him by his seniors at St George's Sunday School, James began to take his role even more seriously. In particular, he became very concerned about the appalling levels of poverty and deprivation he saw amongst his students.

On one level, the Industrial Revolution had brought prosperity to Blackburn. The town was already established as a centre of cotton and wool production, and had been since Flemish weavers settled there in the 15th century. It was well placed to take advantage of the new technology invented by innovators such as James Hargreaves and Richard Arkwright. But with industrialisation came massive population growth, as people gravitated to the busy mill-town looking for work.

This growth continued throughout the 19th century; between 1841 and 1881 the census reports tell us that the population of Blackburn mushroomed from 36,629 to an astonishing 91,958 and over the next ten years alone it would increase by another thirty thousand.

Poverty was common countrywide, but in such a densely populated town, it was so much more visible. Sadly, the general social attitude to poverty was that most poor people were poor through their own fault. Before the 1834 Poor Law Amendment Act, the poor were supported through Parish Relief funds, which were paid for by taxing the wealthier residents of a town – who were often vocal in their disagreement with this arrangement, claiming that they were simply paying people to be lazy and not work. The 1834 Act was intended to change this on a national level, by stating that poor people could only get assistance if they were willing to abandon their homes and go into a workhouse.

This may have relieved the wealthy of their perceived unfair tax burden, but it did nothing to change the centuries-old attitude that the poor were poor through their own fault. Inside a workhouse, husbands were separated from wives and children were separated from their parents. Inmates were poorly fed and forced to work at back-breaking tasks for long hours. The idea was to make life in a workhouse so unpleasant that people would do anything to avoid being sent there. Unsurprisingly, the prospect of being forced to enter the workhouse was universally feared. As it was desperate poverty which led to the workhouse in the first place, any chance of emerging from there to a better life was slim, at best.

A few years later, writing in a fund-raising magazine, James would describe meeting with some of those who had experienced the workhouse environment.

An old man and woman, who have lived in Blackburn over fifty years, sharing the joys and sorrows of life together as man and wife during that long period, are now reduced to extreme want. They are nearly 70 years of age, and all their sons and daughters have died, one of the

24

sons having perished on the battlefield. Sickness overtakes the old man, and want drives them into the workhouse, where the old man and his wife, who have lived together for half-a-century, are separated and compelled to live apart during the five months they remain there. They were, however, allowed the 'great privilege' of seeing one another for half-an-hour once a week. The old man told me he often spent sleepless nights thinking about old times, and crying with sorrow that he was denied the company of the old woman, whose sorrow was equally keen.

The separation proving too severe for them, they left the workhouse last week, and are now much happier living together in a single room, although they have to 'scrat for a living,' glad even to pick up broken bread and fuel from the streets. The old woman's eyes are failing, for one day this week she picked up what she thought was a good lump of coal, but when she had carried it home it proved to be a black brick, so they had to do without fire that evening. I gave the aged couple a few old clothes and a little tea, for which they were very thankful. I have often thought that the law compelling the separation of old couples in the workhouse is very un-English, and certainly contrary to the dictates of humanity. An alteration of the law in this respect is greatly needed.

James gave a further illustration of the unwillingness of the poor to admit themselves to the inhumanities of the workhouse. He described finding an old woman in the depths of poverty, without fire or food. When he suggested that she would be better off in the workhouse, she responded, *'Liberty is sweet. I am not always like this, I can often pick up enough coal on the street to make a fire, and sometimes I get a little food given me, and last week I earned a few coppers to buy tea. They won't give me tea in the workhouse, I would rather die here. Liberty is sweet!'*

By the end of the 19th century, unions and insurances saved many poverty-stricken people from the workhouse, but the threat still hung over many heads when they found themselves unemployed, sick or old. The 1834 Poor Law had done little to ameliorate the actual causes of poverty, which were simply unemployment and low wages. Levels of poverty increased until by the end of the 19th century an astonishing thirty-three per cent of people living in towns were not earning enough to keep their families properly fed and clothed. People could no longer call on the old Parish Relief system as a supplementary source of income whilst they struggled to support themselves again and regain their dignity; their only recourse was to take to crime to avoid incarceration in the dreaded workhouse.

Our current welfare state was still several decades away. It would be almost thirty years until the old-age pension was instigated. In 1880 it fell upon Christian workers, philanthropists and private charities such as the Salvation Army and Dr Barnardo's to do what they could to relieve the suffering they saw all around them.

An entry from James Dixon's diary clearly illustrates how concerned he was at what he was discovering.

24 October 1880. Visited several of my scholars tonight in their homes, was deeply moved by the suffering at the home of one of my scholars (Samuel Collison). The father at home dying being discharged from the Infirmary incurable, in another room of the house was lying the corpse of one of the family of six who had just drawn its last breath two hours before I entered. The mother is sick and the remainder of the household in extreme want. I gave them the two shillings I had in my pocket and spoke some cheering words to the dying man about the blessed hope and consolation of the Gospel.

To the twenty-four-year-old James, seeing such desperate poverty at close quarters must have been shocking, but he was by no means alone in his concern for these desperately poor children. Any Sunday School teacher would witness the same depths of need amongst their pupils and, indeed, Sunday Schools in those pre-welfare state days were well accustomed to providing meals for their charges, and the rudiments of education along with Christian teaching.

A few months after that diary entry, there was a formal meeting of all the Sunday School teachers in the area – more than fifty – where it was decided to set up a Ragged School. In those days there were over two hundred Ragged Schools in England, part of an organised movement to provide basic education such as reading, writing and arithmetic, as well as practical skills such as cookery and needlework and also to provide food and clothing. Of course, these were Christian schools and the children's moral well-being was paramount to their aim. Left uneducated, in the squalor of poverty, these children would, in all likelihood, drift into lives of crime and immorality. The term 'Ragged', of course, referred to the fact that children attending these schools truly were dressed in rags and often went unshod.

Through his involvement with the Sunday Schools, James Dixon had become friends with one John Thomas Walkden and although the two were still only in their early twenties, they jointly took on the bulk of the responsibility of organising the new Blackburn Ragged School. With indefatigable enthusiasm, they enlisted the help of Sunday School teachers from all denominations: Presbyterian, Wesleyan, Congregational and others. They found cheap premises in an old plumber's shop on Leyland Street, which was in bad shape but enough for the immediate purpose and they found a benefactor in Thomas Haworth, who paid the rent for the first three months. Other Sunday School teachers and charitable Blackburn residents donated useful equipment such as wood for building, a stove and a hearth-stone, cupboards, forms and coconut matting, as well as fifty hymn-books and the loan of a harmonium. John Walkden contributed '4 boxes of presents' for a planned 'children's treat' and Mrs Hindle gave apples for the same purpose. Mrs Hindle also paid the gas bill and Mr Dobson and Mr Walton each gave ten hundredweight of coal. Various lady friends contributed cleaning materials and one in particular, a Miss Jane McLellan, gave hat-racks. This is the first mention in the archives of Jane McLellan, who would later become James's wife.

James and John Walkden set about properly researching their project by visiting a Ragged School in Manchester, whose conductor, Mr Johnson, spent the day with them and shared his experience. They returned full of enthusiasm, certain they were up to the challenge. They decided to call their school Leyland Street Ragged School, with

James as secretary and John Walkden as treasurer. The school opened just a week later, on October 22nd 1881 and an incredible hundred and fifty children turned up to be served with coffee and buns. The first proper school meeting was held the next day, a Sunday, and even more children arrived. A hundred and ninety-eight ragged children came to the old plumber's shop, eager for the experience.

James wrote in his diary, *'May God own and bless the work.'*

Now was the time for fund-raising to begin in earnest, because despite the best efforts of friends and supporters, the Ragged School could not be kept open without ready cash to cover the day-to-day expenses of providing hot soup, bread and coffee, quite apart from the costs of giving these deprived children treats such as tea parties and occasional days at the seaside. It is clear that these 'treats' were not regarded purely as luxuries; these children had little joy in their lives, few chances to be children and simply play. Food, clothing, education, religious instruction – all of these were important, but the opportunity to be a child was equally vital. Collections were organised and entertainments laid on, all to raise funds for the Ragged School and its work.

The first Quarterly Report of Leyland Street Ragged School was produced and circulated three months later, on January 22nd 1882. It was intended as a fund-raising publication, so it mostly covered the general topics it was obliged to include, such things as lists of subscriptions and donations, a balance sheet, and a list of officers for the coming year. However, it also included more interesting reading. For instance, it reprinted the Blackburn Times account of the New Year's Day treat given to the children. Both the downstairs and upstairs large rooms had been gaily decorated for the occasion.

'About 360 of the scholars were served with coffee, &c, after which a programme of recitations and songs was gone through simultaneously in both rooms, which were crowded. Mr John Walkden presided in the room on the ground floor, and Mr James Dixon occupied the chair in the upper room. Over 50 of the infant children were each presented with a

toy and an orange. The remainder of the scholars on retiring each received an orange, and all appeared to have spent a very enjoyable meeting.'

The report also described the work the Ragged School had been doing and intended to continue, explaining that, wherever possible, parents as well as children were being helped.

The workers, in their visitation, have been brought into close contact with cases of extreme want and suffering; clothing and other necessaries have been given to the deserving poor. A poor woman (the mother of six children), who has lost the sight of one eye and likely to lose the other also, was on two occasions sent to the Eye Institution in Manchester, the necessary expenses being paid by a Lady Friend, through our Committee.

In addition to teaching the Children in the School and visiting them in their homes (if homes they may be called), it is our intention, when the necessary arrangements can be made, to hold a mid-week service for the Fathers and Mothers and others, who by poverty and a want of suitable clothing are prevented from attending the ordinary Church or Chapel Services.

From a hundred and ninety-eight on the night of the first meeting, to three hundred and sixty just three months later – the number of children wanting to attend the Ragged School continued to grow. The old shop building was overwhelmed. Within months of opening, the search was already under way for more suitable premises. Later in 1882, the Ragged School moved into some disused school buildings attached to St Peter's Church on Bent Street, which Dixon and his friends bought for £150. The bulk of the money for the purchase was collected through subscriptions from sympathisers, with eight local gentlemen contributing a total of £50 and the rest raised by a Bazaar and sale of work. The building was falling down and the crumbling walls had to be shored up, but at least space was now available which was sufficient for the needs of the four hundred and fifty children who wanted to come to the school.

The school provided afternoon and evening sessions, an infant school, twice-weekly mission services and also an adult class, which had a healthy attendance of around seventy-five. Of course, children and adults alike were greatly attracted by the promise of free Sunday breakfasts, free Monday dinners and an annual seaside trip. However, children were also encouraged to join the Band of Hope and its choir, the Fife and Drum Band, and The Boys' Brigade. The School also offered more practical help in the form of a library, a Penny Bank, an old clothes shop and sewing classes, as well as a Benevolent Committee who offered financial assistance in time of need.

In July of 1883, when James was twenty-seven, the Ragged School and all its activities were well established and James approached the Right Honourable Earl of Shaftesbury, asking for his patronage and support in the venture. To be able to use Shaftesbury's name in fund-raising efforts would be immensely valuable, and would give the school added credibility. Shaftesbury had been one of the founders of the Ragged Schools Union and its president for forty years. He had, in fact, spent his whole life working for social reform of various kinds.

Shaftesbury was born in 1801 into a wealthy family. When he entered the House of Commons at the age of twenty-five, it was during a period in history marked by the intense poverty left in the wake of the Industrial Revolution. Those who had worked at home, supplementing their earnings by spinning or weaving, were now out of work. However, the huge factories needed large numbers of workers, so that children, even very young ones, were commonly put to work there, working day shifts and night shifts of such long hours that many died under the strain. Several times, efforts had been made to change such injustice. In 1819, a Bill limited children's hours to sixty-nine hours a week – which was indeed considered a reform – but in reality, the Bill had little effect.

In 1833 Shaftesbury's Ten Hours Bill spoke of his research into these issues, when he had seen large numbers of children crippled and deformed by conditions they had been forced to endure. He said,

'They seemed to me, such were their crooked shapes, like a mass of crooked alphabets.

However, an Act limiting the hours which children could legally work would have ramifications both for industry and the economy of the country, so there was a great deal of opposition. It was not until 1844 that the Ten Hours Act was finally passed. Shaftesbury continued to fight for adjustments to the working hours of children until 1874, spending over thirty years in total to bring them to fruition. He also campaigned against the circumstances of women and children working in coal mines. In 1840, children as young as five were habitually working in mines as beasts of burden, in harness, drawing heavy loads on all fours, suffering stunted growth, a variety of diseases and often, unsurprisingly, death. Children were often bound by 'apprenticeships' to the mine owners, during which time the children would be working simply for board and food. Shaftesbury's work in Parliament put an end to much of this misery. He then went on to address similar, necessary reforms in many other industries.

However, Shaftesbury was also known for his involvement in the Ragged School movement. The movement, though then without a name, had begun as long ago as 1826 when a Home Office meeting sought to address the civil problems in Spitalfields at that time. A contemporary report described *'the dreadful outrages of a gang of lawless thieves, consisting of five or six hundred,'* who regularly bullied and attacked local traders, shopkeepers and the public who happened to run into them when they were running amok stealing food.

Twenty years later, Shaftesbury explored London for himself and found the situation little changed. The poorest lived three families to a house. Gin palaces were uncountable, as were their associated common lodging houses where their drunken customers slept many to a room, with only straw for bedding. In one area he discovered almost a thousand people 'living' in only fourteen houses, whilst in Shoreditch almost two thousand children never attended school. As nearly forty per cent of those held in prisons were illiterate, Shaftesbury saw that the best way of reforming this dire situation was through education.

Shaftesbury resigned his seat in Parliament, became president of the Ragged Schools Union and, two years later, spoke in the House of Lords about the sixty Ragged Schools which had now been set up. His peers in the House queried his wisdom in trying to educate these poor children. What was to be done with all these children, they wondered, once they had been educated? Shaftesbury answered with another question, 'What shall we do with them if they are not?'

By 1883, after forty years' work, Shaftesbury's Ragged School Union had picked up over three hundred thousand children from the streets, educated them, brought them into the Christian faith and sent them into trades and domestic service. A vast majority of these children were now good and honest citizens. Education and a Christian faith, administered by the Ragged Schools, were the reasons.

One can see why James Dixon revered Shaftesbury and why a little hardback biography about the man remains in his family's possession even now. However, at the end of the biography, after all the descriptions of Shaftesbury's efforts on behalf of children working in mills and mines and those in the depths of poverty, there is a note by James which reads, 'What about the poor chimney sweeps?' Always, as James clearly saw, there was more to be done to combat society's injustices against the young.

No wonder, then, that James considered Shaftesbury an ideal patron for his Ragged School. And after receiving James's letter, Shaftesbury wrote back, very cordially agreeing to be a patron, and also enclosing a donation of one pound.

CHAPTER FOUR

On January 1st 1884, the Ragged School children celebrated the New Year with a free breakfast for each of them, which had been generously donated by the daughter of the Mayor of Blackburn. Free breakfasts for an incredible number of poor children – seven hundred and eighteen in total.

It was becoming increasingly obvious that some of the children coming to the Ragged School were not just poor but truly homeless and alone. One evening, as the Ragged School was ending for the night, James was approached by some boys who asked to be allowed to sleep in the school room. They begged to be allowed to sleep on the benches there, so they did not have to sleep in the streets instead. It is not recorded whether James allowed them to stay overnight, but the event did bring home to him the level of need existing amongst these children. James and his colleagues were doing their best, but it was a mere drop in the ocean of want they saw all around them. And so, in 1884, James Dixon and his friends decided to take this charitable work to the next level and provide more permanent accommodation for some of these desperate children.

This was a huge step to take. James was at this point still working full-time, as were most of his friends and supporters. The work he really wanted to achieve, however, could not be done on a purely part-time basis. And so in May 1884, when James was twenty-eight, he came to a momentous decision, which he recorded in his diary.

May 26 – give my whole time to the work of the Ragged School & Boys Brigade, £1-7-6d per week.

His wage was very small; £2 a week less than his previous wage as a joiner. The equivalent today would be around £450 a month. Few people today would be happy with such a wage, especially with no other source of income. In addition, when James said he would give his *'whole time'*, he did not mean nine to five, five days a week. He intended to give his life to this work and this was just the beginning.

Early in 1884, a meeting was held in the Town Hall, involving members of the public as well as wealthy Blackburn residents. The mayor presided. The aim was to establish a home for boys which would be known as a Boys' Rest. The meeting was gratifyingly crowded and there was immense support for the plan. A house at 53 Fielden Street was subsequently rented and set up as a Boys' Rest, opening in April. In September, a similar house was opened as a Girls' Refuge, at 1 Paradise Terrace.

The homes were, in effect, miniature orphanages, operating in just the same way as would Dixon's later full-scale orphanages. Not all the children were truly orphans, but they all came from homes which were chaotic in some degree and struggling with severe poverty. There were always more homeless boys in residence than girls, as the latter were quickly snapped up for domestic service, but their needs were the same: food, shelter, clothing, education and, when they reached the age of fourteen, a job to go to.

Now that the two small homes for boys and girls were open and operating, larger amounts of funding were constantly called for to meet the daily costs of feeding and clothing the young people, paying the bills and paying the wages of the couples employed as superintendents of the houses. To help supplement the donations of the more wealthy supporters, Ragged School boys raised money on the streets by shoeblacking and selling Christian magazines such as *Old Jonathan* and *The Christian Worker*. The practice of sending the boys out on to the streets (where they might once again fall into bad ways) was always recognised as a risky idea and indeed was eventually stopped, but at first it was as good a way as any to raise vital cash to keep the homes operating.

It was at this time that James set about producing his own fund-raising magazine. The style of the writing in early editions – the 'voice' – encourages one to think that James wrote the entire sixteen page magazine himself, although that cannot be certified. The magazine was named *Rags and Rubies*. The frontispiece was from a plate produced by Charles Cattermole, a celebrated artist who was a member of the Royal Academy. The first of its monthly editions went on sale in January 1885. It was, from the first, a successful magazine, selling 6,500 copies in February 1885, 7,500 in April, and 8,400 in June.

The magazine was sold on the streets but, gradually, a regular subscription list was built, ensuring a real source of regular funding. The well-used stencils for printing the address labels for the thousands of envelopes still exist in the orphanage archives. Local businesses also paid for advertising space. The magazine was excellent reading and remains so, carrying a variety of articles, letters, tales of children (anonymous) lately discovered and rescued, Bible texts, and poems of a distinctly Victorian flavour, some gloomy, some cloyingly sweet. Lists of all donations large and small were always included and there were even pages 'For Younger Readers'.

A year later, early in 1886, an edition of *Rags and Rubies* carried an article first published in the Blackburn Telegraph, which describes in detail the interior of the Boys' Rest.

On the left on entering, is the tidy little kitchen in which the Matron and Mr Eccles live, and in which Miss Eccles held a very successful bazaar in aid of the funds of the Institute a few weeks ago. On the right is a large room which seems to be used as a day room by the boys, and at the time of our visit one little fellow, who has the misfortune to be paralysed in his lower limbs, was engaged in tidying up about the fire-place – for Mrs Eccles is bound, with so large a family to attend to, to call upon the boys for assistance. Behind this room is the kitchen, fitted up with a large cooking range, the food when ready is passed through a trap door in the wall to the boys.

Mr Dixon also took me upstairs to see the bedrooms, all of which are large, lofty, clean, and well ventilated, several structural alterations having recently been made to obtain a better supply of pure air, by order of Dr.Pollard, the hon. med. officer. Every boy has a bed to himself. He sleeps upon two mattresses, and his covering, though not luxurious, is warm and comfortable. At the foot of each bed is a locker, in which are stored the personal belongings of the boys, and the key to which he has in his own possession. The walls are adorned with Scripture texts, mottoes, illustrations from almanacs, &c.

Several of the boys were about at the time of our visit, some of them having been at the service at the school, and others having been kept at home to assist in performing the household duties. They all looked clean, healthy and happy, and they responded cheerfully to the questions of Mr Dixon, who has clearly succeeded in winning the affections of the poor little waifs and strays who are dependent upon the Home for shelter, and upon the free meals for a good deal of their sustenance.

Altogether, over 8,000 free meals were supplied last winter, and it is expected that quite as many, if not more, will be given this. The cost of the breakfast is certainly under 1d a head; the dinner of pea-soup and bread is about a penny, or a little over when potatoes are added to the soup; and the supper of coffee, bread and treacle is supplied at a cost of half a penny.

In the pea-soup and potato hash the proportion of meat is two ounces to the pint. The Matron is at liberty to make slight alterations in the diet to suit the seasons, and sometimes the kindness of friends affords the lads a treat, as, for instance, when Mr Eli Heyworth, J.P. sent to the Home the other day for the special use of the inmates a number of rabbits which were greatly relished.

Later in the article, the author included a list of achievements as described by James Dixon in his annual report. It was an impressive account.

In an account of the work the Institution had done during the year, Mr Dixon, at the last annual meeting, said: They had given 8,148 free meals to hungry children, 520 garments, 160 pairs of clogs, 182 tickets for food were given to the sick and poor, 488 tickets for lodgings, 250 children had been provided with a Christmas Dinner, 800 children provided with breakfast on New Year's Day, 1,000 Ragged Scholars had been treated to a holiday in the country, 450 poor children had been taken for a day's trip to the seaside, and 132 boys and girls had passed through the Boys' Home and Girls' Rest, and had been helped in various ways. The School had 1,000 scholars on the roll, of whom 550 were in average attendance. There were also carried on in connection with the Institution mission services, cottage meetings, evening class, singing class, boy's band, tract distribution, night school, Band of Hope, penny bank, free reading-room, library, &c.

The article ended, understandably, with a plea for support, because it was all too easily forgotten that the entire project was funded by charitable gifts and sheer hard work and determination.

In this same edition appeared a letter which had been printed in the local paper – probably written by James – bemoaning the lack of public response. It seems that despite the initial support shown at the first public meeting, the people of Blackburn had let the matter slip from their minds, agreeing that this was valuable work, but trusting that someone else would pay for it to be done.

We cannot but regret that the appeal to the Blackburn public on behalf of the Blackburn Ragged School has been half-heartedly responded to. The sale of work, by means of which it was intended to replenish the empty coffers of the institution, was the occasion for asking for £100. This is not a large sum, but yet only some £74 was the measure of the response.

We have repeatedly placed before the public the claims of the Ragged School; and whilst benevolent and charitable institutions anywhere have always our heartiest sympathy and support, we think an institution which looks after the neglected waifs and strays of a large town is especially deserving of kindly and practical help. But the fact cannot be overlooked that the Blackburn people are very apathetic to the appeals of their Boys' Home. Why they should be so it is difficult to understand. Here we have an institution doing an immense deal of good among the poorer classes. The Home is a shelter for homeless and destitute children, and many a wretched child and homeless orphan has been saved from degradation through its timely agency. Its mission is a hallowed one, which should go straight to the hearts of those who can look on life's cares with sereneness and equanimity.

Pity 'tis that such an institution should go a-begging. It does not say much for the town when the officials of the school have to state that they had the prospect before them of commencing the New Year without a penny of funds. 'Alas for the rarity of Christian charity under the sun!' The institution has a claim upon every one and it would be well if the townspeople brought themselves to realize the duty they have to perform in connection with the homeless children of Blackburn.

In contrast to this remonstration, which was clearly designed to appeal to readers' sense of Christian duty and shame them into contributing, another column in *Rags and Rubies* directed itself entirely at younger readers, speaking with a very different voice. It recorded with charming and gentle humour the efforts of little fund-raisers.

For Little Workers.

During the past month our little friends have been unusually busy helping us in various ways. First we have to record a little Bazaar, held at 37 Bold Street by Miss Annie Buck, 13 years of age, Flora Buck, 11 years of age, Chrissy Bland, 7 years of age. There was a large display of the usual nick-nacks found at bazaars, together with the many useful articles which had been made by the busy fingers of the little girls and their friends.

One table was covered by a large collection of toffy, sweets, &c, presided over by one of the little girls whose customers were so numerous that she never left the table and the scales and weights, until she had weighed out and sold the whole of her stock of sweetmeats.

The little girls were equally busy, and all seemed full of enjoyment in their work to help forward a good cause. I should have told you that weeks before, these little workers might have been seen hastening home from school in the afternoon to get to their work, preparing for the bazaar. *Every spare minute was used up in a useful way; hence the success which attended their efforts, the proceeds amounting to the handsome sum of £2-5-6½d, which was promptly paid over to Mr Dixon, the Superintendent of the Boys' Home.*

Later in this edition, there was a picturesque description of the Christmas *'Free Tea'*, which was laid on for around three hundred poor men and women gathered from the town's common lodging houses.

Let our readers picture to themselves over 300 of the people we have tried to describe, seated in our large mission hall, around several long rows of tables covered with clean white table-cloths, and laden with bread and butter, currant and seed bread, teacakes, &c. A cup and saucer, plate &c are provided for each of the invited guests. The young men bring up the steaming tea-urns and place them along the tables, near to the various ladies who are presiding at the trays. Grace is said and a general attack is then made on the edibles. The plates are speedily emptied but as soon filled again by the young men waiters, who are untiring in their efforts to please the visitors.

By way of adding to the good humour visible all round, Mr Dixon announced from the platform that all present were urged to make a good tea – to eat as much as they liked and drink as much as they pleased, the only limit being that no one was to drink more than sixteen cups of tea on that occasion. This intimation was received with a hearty laugh, which some of the friends in the act of swallowing found a difficulty to control.

This account was followed by the characteristically pithy statement *'One penny provides a warm meal for a hungry child.'*

CHAPTER FIVE

The boys' and girls' Homes which opened in 1884 may have been small, but in terms of the work being done amongst needy children, the concept was very different from the Ragged School's ordinary daily work. Giving out free meals and second-hand clothes to poor children was relatively simple – but providing accommodation on a semi-permanent basis in dedicated children's homes was a more complicated plan, with much greater responsibilities. The children admitted to the Homes were wholly in the care of the Ragged School's board of trustees, who thus bore legal responsibility for the decisions they might take about the children's futures. Indeed, as the years progressed the trustees did find themselves embroiled in a court case which cost them a substantial amount for legal representation and also threatened their personal reputations and that of the Ragged School as a whole. This case became known in the orphanage files as 'The Corless Case'.

Peter Corless and his sister Mary Ann were admitted to the homes in November 1886 at their father's request; their mother had died and he was sick, unable to work, and therefore unable to support his children any longer. He intended to go into the workhouse, but wanted to spare his children that fate. Young Peter Corless was subsequently sent to a refuge in Manchester which was involved with a scheme to send homeless children to a new and better life in Canada. In early 1887 he sailed to a children's home in Ontario, where he was soon adopted. James Dixon had kept in touch with the boy and received letters in which Peter happily described his new home and how pleased he was to be there. Peter's sister Mary Ann was also happily adopted, by a couple in Padiham, near Burnley.

Two years passed and then the children's father, Joseph Corless, demanded that his children be returned to him. This was the first time he had been in touch about his children and so he had no idea that they had both been adopted, let alone that his son was now on the other side of the Atlantic. Understandably, he was angry about this turn of events, but the trustees quite rightly made the point that he had shown no interest in his children since leaving them in the homes two years previously and furthermore he had lied about their religion, knowing that the orphanage was unwilling to take Catholic children into their care.

Nevertheless, Corless took legal advice and late in 1889, took the trustees to court in a case which was guaranteed to make headline news. In the High Court, the presiding judge decided that as young Peter Corless was no longer a child, and as he was half a world away in Canada, he should be allowed to remain there if he so desired. Where Mary Ann was concerned, the judge ruled that she should indeed be returned to her father, whether or not she wished that to happen.

Such a high profile case was bound to be covered in the newspapers. The court hearings and the eventual decision were easy fodder for the journalists who haunted courts in search of good stories to fill their column inches. The judge's decision would be read with interest, as it was not totally in the committee's favour. As well as having to find almost £60 to pay for their legal representation, the committee were obliged to undertake a public relations campaign by writing articles for the local newspapers, in order to explain their actions and retain their reputation and place of trust in the community.

In the event, the judge's decision may have been a good one for young Peter Corless – who in fact had never wanted to come home to England and his father – but it was not so good for Mary Ann. Six months after she had been handed back to her father, James Dixon went to pay one of his regular visits to the family and was told by a neighbour that they had left Blackburn. When he asked exactly where they might have gone, he was given the enigmatic answer, *'There are more than you want to know that.'* Another six months passed before James tracked down Mary Ann and her father, living in a squalid common lodging house in Rawtenstall.

The Ragged School trustees had to accept that it was simply not possible to save all children who deserved a better life. They would come across desperate children on an almost daily basis and they could not always offer help. James Dixon and his colleagues, however, were stoically determined to save as many of these children as they possibly could. In order to achieve this, they needed to take another step forward. The Ragged School and its associated homes were great achievements but James Dixon still harboured an ambition to build full-scale orphanages for the most needy boys and girls. However, it was obvious that this would require more money than the sales of magazines and shoeblacking sessions could possibly provide.

In December 1886, James Dixon demonstrated just how deeply committed he was to his idea by using his savings of £50 to start an Orphanage Fund. His friend and colleague Thomas Hart matched his contribution. Together with their colleagues they started inspecting various sites for their dreamed-of orphanage. The plan submitted to the committee, less than a year later, shows just how large a venture they were planning.

They were searching for a plot of land at least ten acres in size, on which would initially be built an orphanage for about twenty-five boys, with office space. The orphanage would be built of good stone, with large and airy rooms, the dormitories to be heated with hot water pipes. Large and numerous windows were a special stipulation, as were lavatories, bathrooms and a sickroom.

By 1889, the search and the fund-raising efforts had been going on for a frustrating three years. In *Rags and Rubies,* the Ragged School magazine, James often included descriptions of the terrible living conditions he saw during his visits to the slums of Blackburn. The issue from November 1889 painted a very detailed portrait of poverty in all its colours, with story after story of both young and old trying to exist in a culture where poverty was seen as a failing.

Some little time ago I received a telegram from the Governor of Preston prison intimating that a homeless orphan boy had been sent there for 7 days for begging, who was to be discharged next day, and asking me to wire back if I could take the lad into the Home, and he would send him by train. Of course, I replied 'Yes.' I met the boy at the station, and took him into the Home. In reply to my questions he said:-

'I have no father nor mother, sir.'
'Where is your home then?'
'I have no home, sir.'
'What were you sent to prison for?'
'For begging.'
'What made you beg?'
'Because I was hungry.'
"But why didn't you work for bread?'
'I was working, but they sent me away.'
'What for?'
"Because I hadn't my register.'
'And why didn't you get your register?'
'Because I didn't know where to get it, as I didn't know where I was born. So I was sent away, and as I could not get work and could not pay my lodgings, and was very hungry, I asked for a bit of bread at a house, and the policeman saw me, and I was sent to prison.'

This boy had often gone without food, but was never guilty of stealing, and had never been in prison before. He had no home and no friends. He was compelled to break one of two laws. Starving with hunger, he must either break the law of nature and be without food, or break the law of man and beg for a bit of bread, for which crime he is sent to prison to be branded as a gaol-bird. Surely, this is a hard law.

A.B. is from a family of ten, no one working, and almost nothing to eat in the house, except a few crusts I noticed, which had been given by some neighbours.

C.D. When I entered this home I was struck with its neatness and cleanness, and that too in the face of great want and suffering. The mother, an invalid of ten years, sat by the fire with a child in her arms, pale and sickly. The father had lost a limb, and had no work, he was out at the time in search of something to do. They were in great want which the weeping mother felt the more intensely as she had been well brought up in her father's home. Now she fared very badly, for to work she could not, and to beg she was ashamed. The mute suffering of such like really deserving cases is very touching. The little money I left here was well spent.

E.F. It was late on Saturday night when I entered this home. I had often been before, but never saw them in want of the necessaries of life. They were a quiet sober family of four. Sickness and want of employment had reduced them to their last meal, which consisted of a supper made from a few potatoes and a little fat given by a fellow-workman. They were enjoying the meal when I opened the door, and were full of hope that in less than a week they would be at work again. A little timely help was greatly needed here, which they got.

G.H. A mother and her little ones deserted by her husband are in extreme Want, and living in a common lodging-house. This poor woman has seen better days, her early life was spent as a teacher, and subsequently she held the position of a governess in a good family, until her marriage with the man who has now so cruelly deserted her. York was the place where she was left by her husband, from whence she tramped over the country in search of him, carrying the youngest child all the way, until reaching Blackburn, footsore, friendless, and homeless, she is compelled to take refuge anywhere. Her present needs are supplied until more permanent help is got for her.

J.K. One Sunday morning when visiting in the slums a person called my attention to this case of a poor widow and four children. When I entered the house I found the sick woman laid on some straw on the kitchen floor, moaning with pain, where she had lain since two o'clock the previous day, and could not turn herself with pain and weakness. She was poorly clad, her clothing and other things having been sold for bread. After providing food for the family, I went for a doctor, who attended the suffering woman the same day. Subsequently the doctor told me he knew the woman very well, she had recently been fined 5 shillings for not sending her boy to school. 'She had not five pennies in

44

the house,' said the doctor and of course she was sent to prison, seven days hard labour, to live on bread and water. This hardship seemed to have something to do with her present sickness. I have sometimes thought in cases like these it might be better to send the truant boy to an Industrial School rather than send the mother to prison. This poor woman was certainly not without her faults, but I am quite sure her punishment, in this case, was out of all proportion to her offence.

L.M. is the case of a family of six who the previous night had slept on the floor. They had had little or no breakfast, and at the time I entered the mother was trying to make a dinner from some pieces of diseased potatoes the little girls had that morning picked out from among the rubbish (lying on spare ground near) which had been carted there by the scavengers from the Market-place and streets. The Earnings in the house for the week had been 4s 6d as compared with 5s 9½d the week previous.

N.0. is a case of a widow with five children, two of whom are under the doctor with illness. The family were suffering great want, yet the mother was wonderfully cheerful, as was the sick daughter lying on the sofa. But the most lively of all was the eldest lad – aged 17 – who had had to leave work a month ago owing to sickness. He said he intended to be at work again in a month, but gazing at him with sorrowfully discerning eyes I could guess the truth – he would never enter the factory again! Ah! Well, in the country to which he is rapidly journeying he will perhaps find peace. This family needed immediate help.

As if these tales were not enough to stir the heart, James also printed excerpts from letters he had received, calling out for help, asking for the barest of life's necessities, mostly food. A family with seven children and no income, another family with six young ones, a widow with no means of support, a mother of three whose husband had died leaving her penniless, a family where there were nine to keep and only one of them working, the mother of six children deserted by her husband – and a poor woman asking simply for one of her children to have her clogs mended. *'I have three pair of their feet nearly bare all at once.'*

Not all of these poverty-stricken people could be helped – the lack of funds the only reason – but those who were given assistance, and particularly children, readily expressed their gratitude. In this same edition of *Rags and Rubies,* James described how he had come across a *'street boy'* who had no home and no friends, and so had been taken into the boys' home and a few months later sent to a job in the nearby town. The boy had sent a grateful letter and James reprinted it in the magazine.

Mr. Dixon, Dear Sir, I write these few lines to you hoping they will find you in good health as it leaves me at present. I am glad to tell you that I like my place very well and that my Master and Mrs. are very kind to me, and the people where I serve say that I am getting fatter, and my master says that I can either be bound for a few years or go for their own child. I have not much work as there are only three cows, three calves, and one horse to look after, and I am glad to tell you that I can milk cows and am very useful. But Mr. Dixon, I think that I would rather be bound, so that I can have a bit of pocket money every week, or every month. I am glad to tell you that I shall be coming over next week, I should have come on the 28th, only I was very busy. And I think that is all this time, so good night, and God bless you and the good work you are doing. Kisses for you and all the Committee gentlemen, and all the Home boys, and all concerned: here are the kisses... The rest of the page was covered in crosses.

In February 1890, the fledgling Society for the Prevention of Cruelty to Children, less than a decade old and supported by Lord Shaftesbury, held a public meeting and debate in Blackburn Town Hall, during which it was suggested there was not enough reason for a permanent society officer to be appointed in the town. A journalist from the Blackburn Times decided to investigate this assertion more thoroughly by interviewing some of those involved in working with poor children, including James Dixon. It was self-evident that many Blackburn children were suffering through poverty, but the aim of the interview was to find out if there was, in fact, evidence of real cruelty, intended or otherwise. Poverty was one thing; cruelty quite another and the two did not always go hand-in-hand. The Blackburn Times article was in the form of questions and answers. In the reproduction below the journalist is identified as 'BT' and James Dixon as 'JD'.

BT Were you at the meeting addressed by the Rev. Benjamin Waugh, a few days ago?

JD Yes.

BT Is there need for the appointment of an officer in Blackburn?

JD Yes; great need.

BT And could sufficient work be found for him?

JD Ample.

BT Does much cruelty to children exist in Blackburn?

JD Yes, but it is difficult to trace and especially to procure evidence for the purpose of punishing it. I have a case which has been brought to me today, but the party giving me the information would not on any account give evidence in the matter, and in the majority of cases a similar refusal is made. I have not investigated the case, but you may have the particulars as they are given to me. It is the case of a dumb girl, 14 years of age, whose father is dead; and so extreme has been the privation that the child has been seen to gnaw the window frame from hunger. She is kept in a back room, and fed on bread and water. The cruelty is not confined to the inhumanity of the mother, but one day an elder sister put the poker in the fire and asked the child to take hold of the red-hot end of the heated poker. A neighbour, it is stated, gave a piece of bread to this elder sister to take to the dumb child, and received the answer that 'they had not to give it to her as she was living too long.

BT But that case you say you have not investigated and cannot vouch for its accuracy. Tell me of some in which you can personally testify to brutal treatment and absolute neglect.

JD I can give you plenty. There was a woman living with a man not her husband, who had a baby about 12 months old. When I went to this place I found the child inside the house in an orange box, sucking a bottle containing milk, which had thickened and curdled from being kept so long and from the heat. The neighbours told me the mother was drinking, and it was then about five o'clock in the afternoon, and the child had been left all day alone in the house in this state, crying. I borrowed a key from a neighbour and entered the house, when someone said, 'The woman is coming and there will be bother.' This was, however, a false alarm. I went to the authorities, the Police, the School Board, &c., and they kept referring me the one to the other, each in turn stating that it did not come within their province. At length the woman was brought up and sent to prison for two months for her inhuman conduct. While she was in prison I brought two other children of hers, little girls, before the authorities, and had them sent to an industrial school where they would be well treated.

BT Mr. Waugh in his speech was very severe on the system of infantile assurance. Do you know of any case of criminal neglect where there might possibly be a vicious motive in getting rid of children for the sake of handling the money for which they were insured?

JD I cannot say that I do. I have never attempted to trace a case to ascertain whether there had been foul play. I know of a case where insurance money has been paid. It was in the case of a boy ten years old who came to the Ragged School sometimes for a meal. He met me in the street one day, and taking his hand in mine I asked him how he was. He replied, 'Very well,' but I noticed that he had a bad cough. I asked him if he was going to his tea, and he said he had no tea to go to. I then asked if he had had his dinner, and he replied no, he had had nothing since his breakfast that morning at the Ragged School. A fortnight after that, at 11 o'clock on a Saturday night, I was visiting in a yard at the back of one of the streets when an old man said; 'Have you heard about that little boy in the corner that is dying?' On going to look I found the very same little boy I had talked to a fortnight before lying on a miserable bed dying. I spoke to him and prayed with him and subsequently he died. On the Monday after he died I called to see his mother, and found her in the house, along with other women, drunk. The insurance money had been drawn earlier in the day, and with it the mother and these other women were making themselves beastly drunk, the corpse of the little boy lying in the house at the same time. The mother was so dead drunk that she could not speak. I left word with one of the children to tell her mother when she became sober that I had been down, and was very angry, and that I was coming down on the following morning. She met me in Shear Brow before I got to the school the next morning with many apologies. I saw to the child being buried with the unspent insurance money.

BT Is that an isolated case?

JD No, I have no doubt there are dozens of cases of that kind in Blackburn.

BT You cannot say though that in the case you have mentioned there was deliberate ill-treatment of the child with the intention of putting it out of the way in order to get the insurance money?

JD No, I could not say that; I did not investigate so closely to enable me to make any such statement.

BT In one part of his address Mr. Waugh stated that he believed they would have more work in the future among gamblers than among drunkards. Did you agree with him in that opinion?

JD No, not so far as Blackburn is concerned. It might apply to London, but I do not think it applies to Blackburn. The majority of the cases, and the bulk of the cruelty, in Blackburn, I think, arise in the homes of drunkards. Gambling in the sense meant by Mr. Waugh is not so prevalent here as in the places he mentioned.

BT Is there any baby-farming going on in Blackburn?

JD Not that I am aware of. I had once thought of promoting a home for infants in Blackburn, but our work at the Ragged School has been too engrossing. One properly conducted, where operatives could leave their infants in the morning and receive them back in the evening well cared for, would save scores of lives in Blackburn. There is one at

Paisley which is doing a most valuable work. Suitable nurses are engaged and proper medical advice obtained, and the parents pay a few pence per week for the children being left there during the day.

BT Will you give me another case, Mr. Dixon, please – one that will show the especial need for the officer proposed to be appointed, and in which the authorities as at present constituted have thought that it was not their duty to take action from any reason whatever, but especially from the reason that the case did not come within their province?

JD On one occasion I gave a boy a pair of clogs, and found afterwards that the mother had pawned them and was drinking and carrying on dreadfully. I went in search of them, and traced them to a distant part of the town. On enquiry up the entry I was told the woman was a bad woman, and the neighbours would not go into the house with me. After some persuasion they lent me a candle, and one of the men, on being told there was no one in the kitchen, came in. I went upstairs, and in the corner of the back room found this woman and the little boy lying on some straw. The little boy was bare-legged, and shivered from cold and hunger, while the woman was stupidly drunk. It was an awful sight. I said to the man, 'You will come, if I want you, to the Town Hall, to give evidence in the case, won't you?' 'No, no,' said the man. In the room there was a candle burning in a bottle placed among the· straw, and it had almost burnt down to the straw, and possibly, if I had not taken it away, the mother and the child might have been burned. It was an impossible task to awake the mother, so I took the child, who was about five years old, away, leaving word for the woman to be told to come to my office for the boy when she awoke. I took the boy into a cook shop close by and gave him something to eat, and he ate as though he hadn't tasted food for days.

The woman never came near to see after the boy. I tried to get him sent to an industrial school, but failed, as the School Board people said it was scarcely a case for them to deal with, as the boy was too young. I sent to the magistrates' clerk, Mr. Riley, to see if a summons could be taken out against the woman. He did not see how that could be done, certainly not for desertion, as the boy had really been taken from her. I *was recommended to apply to the Board of Guardians, but from none of the authorities could I get help to deal with the case. The authorities have always been ready to assist in these matters as far as they thought their powers permitted them, but in this case none of them thought it was their duty to deal with it. That boy is now in our Boys' Home.*

I found out the mother again, and got her to sign an agreement to pay a shilling a week towards the boy's maintenance, but she has never paid a farthing. If it was not for the drink she could well afford to pay, as when she is not on the spree she can get work at the mill if she likes.

This article clearly showed that the Society for the Prevention of Cruelty to Children did indeed have a place in Blackburn. Cases like the one above, where none of the 'authorities' saw intercession as their duty, were not uncommon. And much as James Dixon and his colleagues purposely sought out such cases, there was only so much help they could offer.

In the same article, James also described the common practice of street beggars 'hiring' very young ragged children from lodging houses to elicit pity, and therefore money, from their audience. He had recently spoken to one such beggar, and offered to take him into the Boys' Home and find him some farm work, but when told that he would not be allowed to use tobacco in the home, the boy had changed his mind and said he could make more money by begging. A few days later, James saw this same boy, with a half-naked child by the hand, barefoot in the snow and singing 'What a friend we have in Jesus.' Passers-by, unaware that the child was being used for the purpose, threw coins in the boy's direction. As James pointed out, the charitable ladies who threw sixpences to such beggars were, albeit unknowingly, supporting one of the worst forms of cruelty. *'No wonder this youth would not work to get an honest living, when he could earn four or five shillings per day by begging in this cruel fashion.'*

It was a good example to illustrate how cruelty to children was not always clearly visible even when it was in plain sight.

CHAPTER SIX

To the workers at the Ragged School, giving their scholars an opportunity to play was almost as important as providing them with food, clothing and the rudiments of an education. For this reason, an annual day at the seaside was an important event and a special fund was set up to raise the necessary funds. Many of the children would never have been so far afield, or seen the sea, or experienced playing on a beach. James described one such event in *Rags and Rubies.* On the great day itself, very early in the morning, the children gathered at the Ragged School for breakfast and then, accompanied by the school's brass band and around thirty teachers and school helpers, processed to the station to board the train which had been especially reserved for them.

'Whoever tipped all this sand here?' asked one of the boys when we got to the sand-hills near the sea shore. 'What a big field!' said another as he gazed for the first time on the broad sea. "Where does all the water come from?' asked a third.

'A, coil fellow, it wur a big brook,' said a little boy, who had been with our Sea-side Trip, to the coal man who was delivering his mother's fuel in the backyard. Several boys and girls asked me the names of the wild flowers growing around the sand-hills at the sea shore, but my knowledge of botany is so limited that this question, like many others the children asked, had to be passed over with a very imperfect answer. I believe the district of Lytham and St. Anne's-on-the-Sea is very rich in its flora; as many as 300 different varieties can be counted.

The day was filled up with donkey rides, sailing, races (with prizes of toys and nuts) and picnic meals, and later one of the teachers entertained the children by making animals out of balloons.

Whilst the day trips brought joy and wonder to these children, of course they were secondary to the practical help which was so sorely needed. An entry from James's diary in early 1889 shows quite clearly the reasons for his growing concern, as well as illustrating in graphic terms the absolute need for a more permanent solution. All through his life, whenever James was asked to explain how the Ragged School and the orphanage dream started, he would describe this particular case.

24 January 1889. Found a little boy (Peter Tomlinson) with his mother lying asleep on some straw in an empty house in Pipemakers Entry, Furthergate. There was absolutely nothing in the house but some straw and a candle in a bottle burning near the straw. The mother was dead drunk, having sold the little boy's clogs for drink.

James later wrote a fuller account which he published in *Rags and Rubies* and indeed, it was described in great detail in the previous chapter, in the newspaper article about the SPCC.

James's discovery of little Peter Tomlinson may have been a pivotal moment but three years had passed since he and Thomas Hart had begun their Orphanage Fund. The time had not been wasted; fund-raising continued apace, but now James began to make serious plans for real forward movement. As vital preparation for the founding of the orphanage, he and his colleague John Thomas Walkden visited several orphanages in other areas, to gather facts, figures, and gain experience from those already involved in running such institutions. In the first months of 1889 they visited Eden's Orphanage in Bolton, which had been operating for around fifteen years, funded through a bequest of £50,000 from James Eden, an industrialist. They also went to Manchester and visited Cheetham's Home and Ardwick Green Industrial School. They visited the Harris Orphanage in Preston, which had only been open for a year. This last was a particularly valuable source of information about building costs, as it was so current.

The Harris Orphanage was designed as a kind of village, with large houses surrounding an open area of grass like a village green. It provided a home for around a hundred and twenty children, the stipulation being that they must have lived within eight miles of

Preston for at least a year. James noted in his diary that the cost of building had been £30,000, and each house held up to twenty-five children. Dormitories sleeping eight children measured twenty-one feet by fifteen feet. James also noted several more practical details: the lavatories were Shanks Patent, all rooms were washed every other day, bedsteads had cost 12s 6d each, the local butcher provided meat for pies at 4d a pound, beef at 6½d per pound, mutton at 7½d per pound and milk was 7d per gallon. James also noted that the Harris Orphanage was funded by an endowment of £75,000, a single bequest from lawyer Edmund Robert Harris, who had inherited vast sums through his family. This was an unimaginable sum if it were to be raised by subscriptions – but James Dixon would not be discouraged.

James was, of course, still heavily involved with the Ragged School and the boys' and girls' homes. One entry in his diary mentions that he had spent the night at the boys' home, covering the duties of Mr and Mrs Eccles, who had left that day, until Mr and Mrs Seddon commenced their duties the next morning. *'I stay all night writing,'* he noted. The mental image this small comment invokes is delightful, as James does seem to have spent an inordinate amount of his time writing. He recorded every child's details in the Admission Books. He recorded daily events in his Occurrences Book. He wrote minutes of committee meetings of the Ragged School and later the orphanage. He wrote monthly editions of the Ragged School magazine. He wrote addresses, lessons, prayers, letters, newspaper articles, pleas for support. One wonders which project he was involved with when he wrote that quick diary note, as his boys slept peacefully upstairs.

It was in this year, 1889, that the site at Wilpshire was finally chosen. A sign was erected upon it proclaiming, in large and definite letters, "ORPHANAGE SITE – £3,000 WANTED". A new group of trustees was set up: fifteen Christian men including James Dixon, his friends John Thomas Walkden and Thomas Hart, and Dr William Pollard, a local doctor who was already providing his services to the Ragged School for free and would continue to do so for the orphanage children for many years to come. These men, all successful in business, were from a variety of backgrounds and trades, from tobacconists, provision dealers and rope-makers to accountants, insurance agents and cotton manufacturers.

The original Trust Deed was signed and sealed on August 9th 1889. The members of the orphanage management committee had to be Protestant, living within a radius of ten miles of Blackburn Town Hall and donors of £25 or upwards. Ten in number, including James Dixon and John Thomas Walkden, the first management committee comprised prominent businessmen and local figures.

From here onwards the minutes of the Ragged School committee meetings are full of matters relating to the planned orphanage building. In June 1889, attention was called *'to the question of disposal of drainage'*. A letter, from the R&R Union, London was read calling attention to provision for fire and pointing out the mistake of having boys and girls together – the first objection was, in practical terms, easy to deal with but the second, while noted, was laid aside for the time being. Naturally it would be better to build two separate orphanages but, for now, to have one would be better than none at all, despite Victorian misgivings. A call was put out inviting architects to tender for the orphanage project and, by July, six sets of plans were brought before the committee for consideration, presented anonymously and identified only by their names: Rags, Rescue, Stet, Thought, Try and Tudor. As the committee lacked the necessary expertise to make a knowledgeable decision between the varied designs, they approached the architectural firm Paley & Austin to act as assessors of the plans. Paley & Austin agreed, generously giving their services for free.

The assessors report was, at first, not encouraging. They did not believe that any of the designs could actually be carried out for the stipulated sum. However, they recommended the design named 'Tudor' as the most suitable for adoption. A point in its favour was that the design was malleable enough to allow for the omission of the whole eastern wing until a later date, and still result in a building suitable for the purpose. Thus, the building could be made more affordable.

The assessors also recommended that the kitchen should be extended a few feet, thus increasing the size of both kitchen and scullery, and that an area designated as a children's playroom should be used instead to house a plunge bath large enough to hold water to a depth of three feet, thus providing a communal bath which could be used separately by girls and boys, under supervision. A suitable playroom could be provided underneath the area then occupied by the bathroom, dining-room and schoolroom. They also suggested the provision of a sickroom and attic bedrooms for servants or staff, as well as using the rest of the roof space for dormitories, which would have beds separated by wooden screens.

The assessors report and the plans for the design 'Tudor' were unanimously accepted by the committee. Only then were the architects responsible revealed to be Briggs & Wolstenholme, a local firm who would later design Blackburn's police courts and fire station.

The next step was the laying of the foundation stone, which would be an event of great ceremony. It was agreed that the event would take place on August 31st and the committee minutes for the whole of that month demonstrate the level of detail involved in planning this historic milestone.

There would first be a procession, leaving the Ragged School at 2.30, passing Salford at 3.00, the cemetery at 3.30, Wilpshire Station at 4.00, finally arriving at the site at 4.30. The mayor had agreed to lay the foundation stone. In preparation, the hedge surrounding the land must be cut and an entrance made in the centre of it. The building of a platform was discussed, to be next to the place where the first stone would be laid but this was deemed unnecessary and planks would be laid around the stone instead. There would be no inscription on the stone but the words Blackburn Orphanage and the date would later be placed on some prominent part of the building. The traditional practice of placing a 'time-capsule' would be carried out – a bottle would be buried beneath the stone, containing coins of the day, up to and including a two shilling piece, also September's edition of the fund-raising magazine *Rags and Rubies*, along with a copy of the last Ragged School annual report, some local newspapers and the mayor's autograph.

The mayor, having performed his ceremonial duty, would then be presented with a ceremonial trowel and mallet by Mr Brierley, on behalf of the committee, and some of the leading townsmen would be asked to move and second a vote of thanks for the mayor. There would, of course, be a collection, under the charge of Mr Roberts.

To advertise the event, fifty wall posters were put up all over Blackburn and, as the next issue of *Rags and Rubies* would contain an engraving of the orphanage and the text of the orphanage Trust Deed, an extra two thousand copies would be printed for distribution in Sunday Schools to stimulate collections.

Before the event, the architects, Messrs Briggs & Wolstenholme, presented each of the ten committee members with a picture of the proposed new orphanage and also gave the committee a bound book of the plans, to be presented to the mayor on the day itself. (This book now resides in Blackburn Museum.)

On August 29th, James arranged an evening prayer meeting, to ask for a blessing on the orphanage plan. The whole week would be observed as a week of prayer for God's blessing. Two days later, on August 31st 1889, the foundation stone for the orphanage was officially laid by the Mayor, Mr John Rutherford. The silver trowel and ivory mallet which were obtained for him to use are still in existence, on permanent display in the entrance hall of the present Orphanage building. Over three thousand people were present at the momentous event.

Now the time had come to select a building firm. The architect's plans were again discussed. The design had been selected because with very little alteration the whole of the East Wing could be omitted, to be built at some point in the future. This was not ideal and several committee members (including James Dixon) felt that the entire building should be constructed, in faith that the cost would be met somehow. There were many discussions, over many months and, as no definite decision could be reached, the general conclusion was that the builder's contract should be worded in such a way that the committee retained the right to decide later, as long as they gave enough notice to the contractor as the building work progressed.

An advertisement calling for tenders from builders was placed in newspapers and nine firms were subsequently invited to submit their estimates. In November of 1889, Mr Hindle's tender was agreed upon. It happened to be the cheapest, but the firm had provided excellent references from their other projects, and the committee were confident that the work would be good. The issue of whether to go ahead with the whole building or leave the East Wing until the money could be raised, remained a thorny one. James Dixon was charged with discussing with Mr Hindle the idea of giving the committee time to consider the issue. What if they decided to go ahead and their decision left them in serious debt? However, James was determined that the East Wing would indeed be built. He argued long and hard for this, even suggesting that the money needed to complete the building should be raised on promissory notes. Understandably, the other committee members were not keen on that idea.

After many months of deep discussion, in March 1890 it was finally resolved that the whole orphanage building, including the East Wing, should indeed be built and that arrangements should be made with the contractor and his sub-contractors to perhaps defer the completion of some parts of the internal work, if necessary, until funds could be found to pay for them. It was a compromise which still went against James's wishes but for the moment, it was the best that could be done. The alternative, that one end of the building should be left unfinished, boarded up against the elements until funds could be found, was simply untenable.

James remained unhappy with this compromise. He was determined that the building entire should be completed, outside and inside and if this meant finding more money, he would do so. Finally, he convinced the committee to allow him to take out a temporary loan of £1,000 on his own, individual, responsibility. Of course, this loan would have first charge on orphanage funds as soon as they were available but the real financial responsibility would lie solely with James. Such was his determination and his faith in the work he had pledged his life to carry out.

The total cost of building the orphanage, originally judged to be roughly £3,000, now stood at nearer to £5,000. With the foundation stone now laid and building work under way, James Dixon and the other committee members began to call for collections from all the church ministers in town. There were raffles, auctions, Town Hall collections, sales of work, bazaars and a concert in the Ragged School. Mr Brierley personally paid for a thousand extra copies of *Rags and Rubies*, to distribute to friends and acquaintances. The London based Refuge & Reformatory Union sent a cheque for £50. The committee also began to seek larger donations, with some success. One of the first and largest was a handsome sum of £500 from Mrs Pickop, wife of a local JP, of Ivy Bank. Early in 1890 James paid a visit to Miss Nancy Derbyshire and her sister Mrs Sarah Sames, and they generously promised to give £400 in two instalments, which would be allocated to pay for the land on which the orphanage would be built.

Later, Mr John Fish, JP, of Southport, who had previously promised to give a tenth of the total building costs, handed over a cheque for £500 towards the furnishing fund – on the understanding that the committee would have to raise the £525 which was still needed in order to finish the building free of debt.

On top of the building costs of £5,000, furnishing the orphanage brought additional expenses. With every committee meeting came another discussion of a seemingly endless list of necessary purchases, duly recorded in the minutes. Fire grates and mantels, tiling for the vestibule and the corridors, a handrail and ironwork for the staircase, wash house fittings, gas fittings, heating, ventilation, electric bells, lead lights, plaster cornices, locks and grilles, towel rails and looking glasses for lavatories, blinds for all the windows (without lace to save on cost), bedsteads, blankets, sheets, quilts, lockers for beside the beds (fifty boxes made of pine with a shelf and a door), two dining tables to measure thirteen feet by six feet by three feet, mugs without handles, plates and basins to be badged Blackburn Orphanage, knives, forks and spoons with flat handles (easier to store), desks and forms, racks for boots and racks for plates, suits for the boys, with peaked caps for the bigger boys and sailor caps for the younger boys on Sundays (plus cheap caps without peaks for everyday wear), towels, slippers – and a bread knife. Tenders for all of these varied items had to be invited, examined, discussed and contracts decided upon.

Costs continued to pile up, but James never lost heart. He was a man of great faith, and always believed that if he was doing God's work, somehow God would make sure that the work was carried out. His faith was justified many times over as wealthy and influential Blackburn residents offered their financial support to his huge project. In October of that year, Mrs Yerburgh donated the vast sum of £1,000 and James was immensely relieved. He wrote in *Rags and Rubies*:

My heart actually leaped for joy on opening the letter box on Friday morning and finding Mrs. Yerburgh's letter with £1,000 cheque enclosed. This, added to the other handsome donations already received gives us cause for great thankfulness. I could not help breathing a prayer to God, the giver of all good, for thus influencing the hearts of those to whom He has given the silver and the gold, to give it freely to the Lord's work, and to help forward the building of the Orphanage, which has already been owned and blessed by Him who hath said He will be a Father to the fatherless.

CHAPTER SEVEN

Fund-raising continued apace as the first orphanage building was constructed brick by brick. Alongside all this activity, work still continued at the Ragged School, where the building was also in sad need of financial investment. Early in 1891, the trustees received word that Mr Ainsworth, a supporter of the work, had died and left £2,000 to the Ragged School. This was welcome news, as there was an urgent need for a new infants' room, an office, better lavatories, a new roof, new stairs, better heating and much more. Plans for the proposed alterations to the Ragged School were duly prepared, laid before the committee and fully explained by Mr Briggs, the architect responsible. However, it was agreed that nothing should be done just then. It was hoped that the building should be not just improved, but extended, if it was possible to buy some of the cottages adjoining the school. These cottages were owned by Colonel Jackson and he must be contacted.

Thankfully, Colonel Jackson was amenable to the idea of selling and offered a total of twelve cottages in Bent Street, and their land, free of ground rent. The Ainsworth Bequest would, naturally, be essential for such major works to be carried out. Unfortunately, the trustees had no idea that the promised bequest would not be finally awarded until several years later. The minutes of the committee mention the Ainsworth Bequest repeatedly for months which stretched into years. On one occasion a deputation of Sunday School teachers came before the committee, so concerned were they that the very necessary improvements to the buildings were taking years to happen. At last, the money arrived, and the cottages were bought. Some were demolished and the construction of a larger Ragged School began.

Early in 1891, a small eight page pamphlet was published, entitled *'Blackburn Ragged School, And How It Was Founded.'* Less formal than the usual Annual Reports, this was an informative little piece explaining how the Ragged School came to be and detailing the impressive catalogue of work it had achieved. It ended, naturally, with a paragraph about the orphanage and the necessity for it. It was not a blatant plea for funds, but a gentle account, inspiring sympathy for the children and appreciation for the humility of those working to take care of them. It was designed to encourage readers to give of their own accord. Written by one H Coard, it was reprinted from the Blackburn Standard and Weekly Express, in which it had first appeared.

The article began with a brief and poetic description of how the very first Ragged School came into being, the Ragged School Union growing from the efforts of John Pounds, a *'poor, illiterate, deformed cobbler... whose unostentatious philanthropy raised him, unconsciously, to the high dignity of the title of Founder of Ragged Schools.'* He was uneducated but able to teach the basics of reading, writing, and arithmetic. He passed this basic wisdom on to hundreds of poor children in an effort to help them lift themselves out of poverty and find better lives. He also handed out cups of tea to all and sundry and visited the sick with soup and broth. It was his selfless example which inspired the foundation of the Ragged School Union and certainly his simple philosophy – to help those too poor to help themselves – was shared by James Dixon and all his friends and colleagues.

The pamphlet went on to describe the work of James's own Ragged School, Boys' Rest and Girls' Refuge, in the decade since the first school had opened in the plumber's shop. Now, the article stated, Sunday Schools were held in the afternoons and evenings, every week. The number of scholars had grown to over a thousand. The Boys' Rest provided accommodation for twenty boys, but was always crowded, and there were currently twenty-seven boys in residence. The Girls' Refuge was supposed to cater for four girls but again, usually had more residents than was officially sanctioned by the Inspectors. In the previous year, a total of a hundred and ninety-five children had been helped by these two small Homes. This was a clear indicator of the pressing need for a proper, full-scale orphanage.

In addition to helping children, during the winter months two hundred poor men and women benefitted from free breakfasts of bread, margarine, and coffee. Every Tuesday, a lunch of vegetable soup and bread was served to two hundred poor children. About five gallons more soup was distributed by hand to those too sick to leave their homes. Once a month a temperance meeting was held and, every Sunday, religious services were held for as many of the parents as could be persuaded to come along.

The article drove its point home by listing an impressive tally of achievements from its ten years of work.

50,000 tracts distributed; 15,000 visits made to the homes of the poor in the borough; 10,000 free meals given (principally to children); 1,250 new and second-hand articles of clothing, clogs, &c given; 1,000 scholars on the roll of the Sunday School; 480 scholars in average attendance receiving religious training; 800 children provided with breakfast on New Year's Day; 410 children provided with Christmas Dinner; 220 lodging-house men and women provided with a free tea; 440 times food &c, given to the sick and poor at their own homes; 900 scholars treated to half-day in the country; 466 poor children taken for a day to the sea-side; 600 quarts of warm soup sent to the homes of the poor, sick, and feeble ones; 195 boys and girls dealt with at the Home and Refuge; 50 boys and girls placed in situations. Band of Hope, temperance and religious meetings, penny bank, band, choir, and children's services are also actively carried on. The sick among those associated with the Institution are generously treated by Dr Pollard, who is its honorary Medical Officer.

By the time this pamphlet was published, a date was being planned for the grand opening of the orphanage. But another great event was to take place, just beforehand. James Dixon's friendship with Jane McLellan had grown as they had laboured to open the Ragged School, the homes and now the orphanage. Jane shared James's ambitions about the orphanage and although she may not have fully realised the extent of the constant work which would be involved in being matron and mother to so many children, James could not have wished for a better partner in his new venture. And so, on March 17th 1891, James and Jane were married.

The couple were married at St George's Church, by their friend the Rev Dr Grosart. Naturally the children took part in the wedding celebrations. A week after the ceremony, there was a celebratory tea party at the Ragged School, after which James and Jane were presented with *'a handsome desk in walnut'*. The next evening James and Jane treated the home boys and girls to a tea party and entertainment, in celebration of their marriage.

The Dixons would begin their married life in the orphanage and would stay there for decades to come.

CHAPTER EIGHT

In the twelve months before the orphanage opened, the question of religious education for the orphanage children repeatedly raised its head. It was a question which had always caused a great deal of concern. Even in the early days of the Ragged School, Catholic clergy had objected to the school's practice of offering free breakfasts on Sunday mornings, claiming this would keep Catholic children away from the church services. James's response to this criticism was that those partaking of free breakfasts were unlikely to be churchgoers, if for no other reason than they had no Sunday clothes. When it became apparent that James and the committee would be opening an orphanage and taking full responsibility for so many children, more questions were urgently asked. The committee was forced to make a definitive decision on its protocol regarding Catholic children. They resolved that any such children coming to their attention would be referred to the relevant Catholic priest, so that he could give the case his consideration and search for alternatives before agreeing to admission.

In August 1890, the committee was also approached by the Rev J A Rushton, the Church of England's Chapter Clerk, who wrote with concerns about the children's intended religious education. He was duly informed that the committee was bound by the Trust Deed and that *'the committee will be guided by clause 10, which directs that all children admitted therein will be trained in the Protestant faith and the Holy Bible shall be the ground work of all religious teaching. The Committee have no objection to the children attending Divine Service in Salesbury Parish Church and as the national day school of the Parish is comparatively near it is the intention of the Committee to arrange for the children to attend it.'*

In December, they were obliged to reply to more queries from the Rev J A Rushton about how they intended to handle cases where guardians of children requested that they be brought up in one particular faith. Their reply was that *'in every case where the proper guardian of any orphan when admitted shall express a desire for distinctive church teaching for such orphan such wish will be duly respected.'*

This brought a response from the Rt Rev Bishop Cromer Roberts himself, questioning the wisdom and authority of the committee in these matters and expressing his wish that the orphanage should ally itself to the Church of England exclusively. James Dixon wrote a personal reply, making it clear that the views contained therein were his alone and not a committee statement and in which he made his feelings quite clear.

You can quite understand how unwise we would be if we pledged ourselves to exclusive Church of England teaching, or Congregational, or Wesleyan, or Baptist, or Presbyterian, or any other section of the Protestant Churches. We intend to send the whole of the children to Salesbury Church and School, but we could not exclude, say, the Rev Davies, Dr Grosart or other well-known good men addressing the children at the Orphanage.

The Trust says we have to go on Unsectarian lines and exclude Roman Catholics only, surely all sections of the Protestant Church might unite in this. When you remember that six of the ten gentlemen who compose our Committee are churchmen, I think you will agree with me that the interests of church children will be well-looked after. In my opinion there can be no objection to the orphans of church-people, if desired, being prepared for confirmation by the Vicar of Salesbury, but to exclude non-conformist ministers addressing the assembled children in the Orphanage would be unfair. Church clergy and non-conformist ministers will both be asked to speak to the children & teach them to love Jesus.

I am, yours faithfully, James Dixon.

Only a few months later, in February of 1891, the committee received an application from the Catholic Rev Father O'Hannahagan, asking to be given custody of three orphans by the name of Crook, as they were

Catholic children. Despite the Trust statement that Roman Catholics would be excluded, the two girls and their brother had been in the homes for a while and they were doing well. The committee was very unwilling simply to hand the children over to Father O'Hannahagan, now that they had some much needed stability in their lives. The committee's considered response was to request proof of the priest's authority in this matter, including proper consent from any legal guardians of the children. This gave James, as secretary, time to discuss the matter with the relatives himself and also to consult a solicitor. In the event, the children's relatives actually preferred that the children should remain where they were and were happy to sign a statement to this effect. And so, despite Father O'Hannahagan's misgivings, the case was closed.

On May 21st 1891, now James and Jane were married, they were officially appointed to be superintendent and matron of the orphanage. James Dixon would also be general secretary and their remuneration would be a joint £75, plus board. The grand opening of the orphanage was arranged for July 23rd and once again the committee's Minute Book was full of the myriad details which had to be decided upon.

In May, Mrs Pickop of Ivy bank was asked to perform the opening ceremony. Mrs Pickop had been one of the first donors to the project, ever since the day when she had driven past the building site in her carriage and stopped to learn more about the planned orphanage. One of the Annual Reports tells the story.

She became interested, and after a chat with Mr Dixon, gave £50 towards the building fund. Thenceforth she would often drive out to watch the progress of the building, and the founder's delight may be imagined when she handed him one day a cheque for £500, with the remark that she was glad a building worthy of the town was being erected. The same lady agreed to make up the balance of money required to complete the Home, so that it could be declared open free of debt.

A ceremonial silver key would be bought at Mr Sagar's jewellers on Church Street and either Mr or Mrs Tom Parkinson would present it to Mrs Pickop. The key would be engraved, *'Presented to Mrs John Pickop, Ivy Bank, on the occasion of her opening the Blackburn Orphanage, 23rd July 1891'*, and until the day of the opening would be displayed in Mr Sagar's shop window, to advertise the great event.

Messrs King & Blackburn's shop window also served as an advertisement for the opening, as they had designed a tasteful display of the hundreds of quilts and blankets which would later come to the orphanage, together with a girl's uniform of dress, cape, cloak and hat. The ceremony would be presided over by Mr Yerburgh, with either Mr Heyworth or Mr Tom Hart to preside if Mr Yerburgh, who had a busy schedule, could not attend. Mr Walkden and Mr Brierley would thank Mr Yerburgh and either the Bishop or the Archdeacon would give a suitable Bible reading. Dr Grosart would offer a dedicatory prayer. James Dixon would make a statement, the Revs P H Hart and A Foster would give out hymn sheets and the Revs Slack and Shillito would thank the Chairman. A public tea was planned, to be held in Salesbury School in preference to the town hall.

All these plans were thrown into turmoil on June 19th, when Mrs Pickop unexpectedly died. James Dixon visited her son and daughter-in-law, Mr and Mrs Frederick Pickop, to offer his sincere condolences and also to invite them to open the orphanage instead. Understandably neither of them felt they could take part, as the date was so soon after Mrs Pickop's death. However, Mr Pickop told James of a letter he had found after his mother's death, in which she stated that she wished the entire balance of her bank account – some £1,700 – to be devoted to the orphanage. This was very welcome news because the money would allow the committee to open the orphanage free of debt. What was left would be used to start an Endowment Fund.

With less than a month to go, the committee found themselves casting about for a suitable, notable, person to open the orphanage. Mrs Yerburgh was the next to be invited but unfortunately, she could not make herself available on the arranged date. The committee drew up a further list of three candidates: Miss Nancy Derbyshire, and if she were not available, Mrs Shackleton and, if neither could attend, Mrs Tom Hart. Fortunately, Miss Derbyshire, who had donated so graciously to the orphanage funds, was available and more than willing to perform the duty asked of her.

On July 7th, the orphanage committee held a special meeting to compile a list of boys and girls to be considered for transfer from the Boys' Rest and the Girls' Refuge to the orphanage; twenty children in total were listed, of whom fifteen were boys. A week later, more cases were considered and nine boys and five girls were added to the list. Some of these children were truly orphans but many had mothers or fathers still living that simply could not care for them, whether through sickness or poverty. After much discussion, thirty-two of these children were accepted for admission to the new orphanage.

A committee meeting on July 10th agreed to appoint staff for the orphanage – Miss Robinson was appointed needlewoman at a salary of £18 per year, Mrs Lancaster was appointed cook at £16, Miss Collison was taken on as a general servant at £13 and Joseph Harrison given the post of yardsman at £15. It was also agreed to accept Mr Haworth's tender to supply milk at two shillings per dozen quarts and a lactometer should be bought to test the milk against diseases such as tuberculosis and brucellosis which were then thought to be transmitted through untreated milk. Nightshirts and other undergarments should be bought from Mr S Pickering and a wringing machine should be bought from Mr Mercer's.

Also, importantly, the committee agreed to send a letter to Mr Hindle, the orphanage contractor, asking him to make the building of the boundary wall a priority, employing more men on the job if necessary, so it would be finished on Opening Day.

Finally, a long set of Rules and Regulations were read and passed:

1. *The object of the Institution is to receive Orphan Boys and Girls, children of Widows, or other helpless and destitute children,*

between ages of 4 and 12 years, and to provide them with board, clothing, and education, until the boys have reached 14 or 15 years of age, and the girls 15 or 16, at the discretion of the Committee.

2. Applications are considered at meetings of the Committee with whom alone is vested the election of children according to the Trust Deed.

3. A preference is given to children who have lost both parents, but children who have lost one parent may also be admitted. If the accommodation or the funds are inadequate to provide for the whole of the eligible candidates, the selection rests with the Committee.

4. Every child previous to admission must have been vaccinated.

5. The friends and relatives of the children are informed that each child is admitted on the understanding that they will be prepared to remove such child when required to do so by writing, or whenever, according to the rules of the Institution, the child shall no longer be entitled to participate in the benefits thereof. Also that at any time a surviving parent or relative of the orphan may be able to pay any part of the cost of maintenance and education of such orphan they shall enter into an undertaking so to do at the time of admission of the child.

6. The following clothing is to be provided by the child's relatives and friends, and handed to the matron on the child's admission: Boy – 2 day shirts, 2 night shirts, 2 pocket handkerchiefs, 2 pairs socks, 2 flannel singlets. Girl – 2 chemises, 2 night dresses, 2 flannel petticoats, 2 white pocket handkerchiefs, 2 pairs stockings, 2 flannel singlets.

7. The friends and relatives of the children are permitted to visit them on the first Monday of every month between the hours of 2 and 4. Each child is allowed a short holiday once a year, provided that his or her conduct has been good, and that his

friends are able to receive and take proper care of him. In the case of the serious illness of any child the friends will be informed.

8. Persons desirous of obtaining the admission of children into the Orphanage will be supplied with forms on application to the Secretary, which must be correctly filled in and returned, together with a certificate or other satisfactory evidence of the date of the child's birth. A form of medical certificate will be supplied by the Secretary, which must be filled up by a duly qualified medical man, who will examine and certify as to the health of the child. This form must be sent in with the application to the Secretary.

9. The religious instruction in the Institution is Unsectarian in character. The children will attend Salesbury Parish Church on Sunday mornings and the nearest Nonconformist Chapel on Sunday evenings.

10. The boys and girls who are strong enough are appointed in turn to assist in the work of the house – not interfering with their education, care being taken that a sufficient time is given them for healthy recreation. The work of the boys is confined chiefly to keeping the play-rooms, yard, &c, clean, making their own beds, assisting in the boiler-house, gardening, keeping the Orphanage grounds tidy, &c. The girls are taught needlework, and at the age of 13 or 14, when they have passed their standard at school, they shall devote their whole time to domestic work, so as to be able at the age of 15 to cook any ordinary meal, wash and iron, cut out and make garments, and perform other household duties which are likely to prove useful to them in after life. Girls going out to service will be provided with an outfit, which becomes their own property after six months' satisfactory service in the same situation. Each boy is provided with a suitable outfit when he is sent from the Orphanage to a situation, which becomes his own property after six months good conduct in a situation.

11. *The Orphanage is open to visitors from 10 am to 6 pm on Thursdays. All visitors to sign their names in the book kept for that purpose. The children's service in the School-room, at 2.30 on Sunday afternoons, will also be open to visitors.*

12. *Persons wishing to visit the Orphanage at other times should make application in writing to the Superintendent and Secretary, from whom any further information about the Institution may be obtained.*

On August 5th 1891, the orphanage was officially opened. James and his new wife, Jane, officially moved into the orphanage as a married couple and also as superintendent and matron. They had actually taken up residence a week before the building officially opened and this milestone is the first event recorded in James Dixon's desk diary, his 'Occurrences' register. They had spent the week making the rest of the house ready to receive its first brood of children.

Adolphus Curran is commonly said to be the first boy to be admitted to the orphanage and, indeed, he is registered as child number 1 in the Boys' Admittance Book. In fact he was just one of the twenty-three boys and ten girls who were all admitted on August 5th.

Adolphus Curran was born in October 1878, so would have been almost thirteen when he came into the orphanage. However, along with his eight-year-old brother Arthur, Adolphus had been in the Boys' Rest since their father died in March 1889 of lung disease. This may have been connected with his trade of 'paper stainer'. The boys' mother had died when Adolphus was only seven years old and Arthur only two. There were three elder brothers, John and James living away from Blackburn and fourteen-year-old Alfred, who was living with a grandmother who was too poor to support two more growing boys.

Similar stories were registered in the Admittance Book about the other children who became the first residents of the orphanage. The children came from a total of twenty-one families.

Three children from the Crook family, John, Catherine and Mary, had been taken into refuge after both their parents had died. Their father had succumbed to pneumonia in 1890 and they lost their mother a year later, after an operation to remove a needle which had been in her body for several years went badly wrong. There were seven children altogether, but the older ones were already looking after themselves. A baby sister had been adopted by a man and his wife who were without a family of their own, but they could not take more of the children.

Charles Holden was eleven years old, the middle child of five, whose father, a weaver, had died when Charles was only three. His mother had struggled to support her children for seven more years before she died herself. The eldest boy was already working as a farm labourer and living away from home and the eldest girl was married but it still left the three youngest children without anyone to care for them. Charles's younger brother and sister were taken in by an aunt. She could not afford to take Charles as well.

William Hirst's father, a gardener, died when he was six and his mother when he was seven. He did have an elder sister and an aunt, but neither was prepared to take him in.

Fred and Jacob Aspin lost their father in 1890 and their widowed mother was left with seven children to take care of. The two eldest were working in the cotton mill but there were five others aged ten, seven, five, three and one. Fred and Jacob, the eldest of the five, were taken in to give her some relief.

Emanuel and Alfred Burns had lost their father to heart disease and their mother had disappeared. According to reports she was living in a common lodging house.

George Albeck's parents were German and had lived in London until George's father died, leaving his mother with four-year-old George, a two-year-old sister and a baby. For reasons unknown they had moved to Lancashire where George's mother did her best to support her family but could only find low-paid work as a cleaner. However, she was not coping, so George was taken into the Boys' Home to lessen her burden.

Thomas Hall, eleven, was from a similar poverty-stricken family. His father was a boilermaker and had been killed in a terrible accident at his work. His grief-stricken mother, left in poverty, had several younger children to support.

Thomas Boyes had lost his mother when he was seven. She had come from a respectable family and had brought to her marriage a small fortune of £800. The farmer she married had taken to drink, spent all her money and reduced them to poverty, eventually deserting them. After his mother died, his father had been located and promptly imprisoned for neglect of his family. His elder sister had married and his elder brother was an apprentice joiner. Neither of them could take Thomas so he was effectively homeless.

Thomas Hindle had lost his father when he was just five years old and now, at thirteen, was on his own. His mother was *'supposed to be living but her whereabouts is not known'*. His ten-year-old sister was living with a lady in Darwen but poor Thomas was alone in the world.

John Charles Haworth was another thirteen-year-old, similarly alone in the world. His father was assumed to be dead but he didn't know when or where and whilst his mother was supposed to be alive, she was just as untraceable. He had an older sister, whom he thought was in service – somewhere.

Eight-year-old John Lancaster was a little more fortunate. His father had died when he was six, but his mother had managed to continue to support him. When John was moved from the Boys' Home to the orphanage, his mother came with him, employed as cook.

David Dyson was ten and had lost his mother five years before. His father had tried to support him but had eventually abandoned him and disappeared. He did have an elder sister but she was in service and could not help him.

Stephen and William Styzaker, brothers of nine and seven, had lost their mother in 1886. Their father and sister were living with their grandmother in the Union Buildings, which were infamously cramped and poverty-stricken houses.

Peter and Winifred Tomlinson, nine and thirteen, had lost their father seven years previously. Two elder brothers had found work and left home but their mother was a heavy drinker and incapable of taking care of her two remaining children properly.

Ten-year-old Thomas Heaton's drunkard father had disappeared and his mother had died in 1890. His three sisters, thirteen, nine and seven, had been taken in by various friends and relatives but no-one was prepared to take young Thomas.

Brothers John and Thomas McGee, eight and ten, were the children of a pedlar who had managed to support them until his death three years previously. Their mother had vanished. Their four-year-old sister was living with a relative but the boys were homeless. (Three years later, a note in their records stated that their mother had been located and had died. The inquest's verdict was *'death through excessive drinking'*.)

Nine-year-old John Mayman had lost his father and then been abandoned by his mother, who had disappeared.

Fernandez and Rachel Taylor, sisters aged eight and six, were from a large family. Their father had died in the lunatic asylum two years previously and their mother was struggling to take care of them and another sibling, as well as five other children from their father's first marriage.

Edith and Eliza Urmston, eleven and four, had lost both their parents. They did have a grandfather and an uncle but neither of them was able to care for the two little girls.

Twelve-year-old Cecilia Boyd's father was in penal servitude for life. Her mother was a charwoman, stricken by poverty and unable to cope.

Elizabeth Killeen was nine and no-one knew the whereabouts of her parents. She had no siblings, and no relatives.

Alice Roper, aged twelve, knew her parents were dead but could not tell when. Like Elizabeth, she was alone in the world.

These thirty-two children were the first to take residence in the orphanage. In total, the building could accommodate around fifty needy children. Needless to say, the empty spaces would soon be filled.

Within the walls of the orphanage, there was of necessity a strict time-table. As matron, Jane Dixon was responsible for the smooth running of this extended family. A daily routine – including playtimes – was essential.

At 6.30 every morning, the children would get up, have a wash, get dressed and make their beds. From 7.00 until 7.45 was a designated playtime, before prayers and breakfast at 8.00. At 8.30 the children lined up for inspection before setting out on their walk to school in nearby Salesbury. At 12.00 they would head back to the orphanage for dinner and a wash, then back to school for the afternoon, from 1.00 to 4.00. At 5.30 they would wash again before supper at 6.00 and then, when they had cleaned their boots or clogs, there was more playtime. At 8.00 they would do any necessary preparation for their school lessons (or a plunge-bath on Saturdays), before prayers at 8.15 and bedtime at 8.30.

The orphanage diet was basic and bread was a main part. The available funds did not allow for expensive or frivolous food. Breakfast every day was bread and butter and a half pint of coffee or cocoa. Supper was more bread, with, depending on the day, butter, dripping or treacle, washed down with tea. The seven daily dinner dishes were minced beef pie with a potato crust, vegetable soup, fish and potatoes, roast meat and vegetables, haricot beans and gravy, Irish stew, bacon and cheese. Dinner-time puddings such as jam tarts, rice, tapioca or suet puddings were simple but filling. Jane Dixon did make seasonal changes, assuming that funds allowed, but in any case, children never went hungry. At every meal, bread was allowed *'without limit'*.

Within weeks of the orphanage opening its doors, new children began to arrive. An initial application form was completed for each child, giving as much information about the child and the family as was possible. It stated whether the child was being recommended by a relative, a friend, a local church member or some other sympathetic person. Each application was accompanied by a medical certificate, which would be completed by either the child's family doctor or Dr Pollard, who gave his services to the orphanage without charge. Amazingly, the majority of these application forms and medical certificates still survive. The details contained in them would later be copied up into the Admittance Books – huge leather-bound ledgers, specially printed with two pages for each child. Each page was numbered, the number starting with a B for the boys' register and G for the girls'. Each child's name was written into an alphabetical index at the front of the book with the page number written alongside so that their record could easily be found.

Here would be recorded the child's name, age, date of birth if it was known and the family situation which necessitated admission to the orphanage. Here are laid bare all the details of Blackburn's poor of the 1890s – sickness, alcoholism, lack of employment or abandonment. Names and addresses of surviving parents, elder siblings, grandparents and aunts and uncles, would all be recorded here, along with the reasons why these people could not look after the unfortunate child themselves.

Also recorded would be the date the child left the orphanage, either discharged to a relative's care or, more usually, when a child reached the age of fourteen, to take a job. Details of the job that had been found for him or her and the address of the employer would be noted carefully. On the facing page, headed *'Subsequent Information'*, would be recorded a variety of dated information and events, from discoveries of previously unknown relatives, or a succession of jobs a child might hold in the future, to records of letters received from grown children in their successful adult lives.

James also wrote regularly in the Occurrences Book, which was in effect a desk diary. This large red ledger book was used as a log of events in the orphanage, right from the day James and Jane moved in. It continued to be used throughout the life of the orphanage – the last entry is dated September 12th 1983. By its very nature, the Occurrences Book contains only a brief account of happenings but even so, the picture it paints is vivid and colourful. It records every stage of the orphanage's development, the successes when children grew up and were placed in situations which suited them, the hubbub when measles or scarlet fever took hold and the sickroom was filled to capacity, the sadness when a sick child lost their hold on life and was carried to the church for the final time by children who had shared their last days.

The Occurrences Book was also used to record reports from a variety of school inspectors. The first such inspection was on September 23rd, a matter of weeks after the orphanage opened. The inspector was from the Reformatory and Refuge Union, which had been founded in 1856 and had ninety homes throughout the country to shelter and help the fallen, destitute and neglected, particularly women and children. It was important to have favourable reports from all such bodies to maintain the reputation of the orphanage. The inspector looked over the buildings and the books, stayed overnight, and in the morning he gave tests to the school age children before leaving after lunch. His report, a copy of which reached the orphanage a fortnight later, was most favourable. He said:

I visited this Institution on Thursday the 24th of September last and found everything in perfect order – at least as far as a new building can be made so shortly after its first occupation. All the rooms are lofty, well-ventilated and warmed. The Sanitary arrangements are of the most improved kind and no expense has been spared to make the building adapted to the purpose to which it is put and worthy (of) the town of Blackburn.

The building provides accommodation for forty-five children: fifteen girls and forty boys, at the present there are only 35 in residence, eleven of whom are girls and twenty four boys. The want of funds prevent the Committee from filling up the vacancies at present.

All the children attend the Elementary School in the Township, six as half-timers the rest as whole-timers, and are being prepared for the Government Examination in February next; they have only attended school for a few weeks.

These were tested in Arithmetic according to the standards IV, III, II and I. Six did well, six did fairly and eight did badly. Many of the children do not know their tables and so use their fingers for counting. This defect should be remedied. I gave standards IV and III two exercises in Dictation including the spelling of words sounding alike but spelled differently; the result was on the whole very creditable. With careful teaching during the next few months the children will I think make a good pass in February next.

I was very much pleased with all I saw in this new Home, and feel sure that it will accomplish great good in the future. Joseph Hassell, AKCL Examiner.

Six months later, in March 1892, Mr Hassell made another visit and submitted another report, commenting that the children's educational standards had markedly improved, and commented:

All the children looked healthy and happy. They are evidently well-cared for by Mr & Mrs Dixon, whose aim is to infuse into the Home a family spirit, and in this they are eminently successful, all the arrangements of the Home are excellent in every way.

James Dixon and his friend and colleague John Thomas Walkden

Fund-raising advertisement showing the planned orphanage buildings

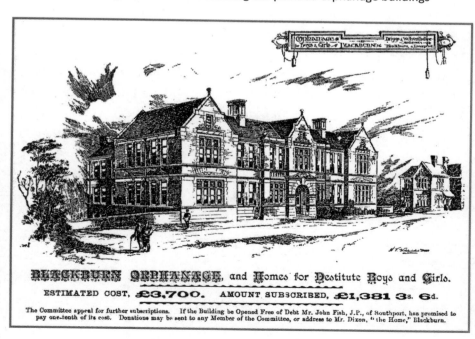

The original orphanage building, opened in 1891

The second building, for girls, opened in 1904

(left) James Dixon and a staff-member on the steps of the original building

(right) James and Jane Dixon on the steps of the girls orphanage

(below) Promotional postcard showing five original Trustees

Group photographs of the Orphanage Boys

Inside the Orphanage - Helping with the baking

In the Dining Room

Making bread and jam for tea

Planting potatoes

Jane Dixon, Matron

Mrs Wilbraham, Cook

Mr and Mrs Taylor, Assistants

Other staff members

Portraits of James Dixon and Jane Dixon
presented on the occasion of their Silver Wedding and James' 60th birthday

The whole Orphanage, assembled for a celebration

CHAPTER NINE

Obviously, James and Jane could not look after so many children without help. Children were expected to do their share of household chores, but a qualified cook was needed right from the start, as well as someone to oversee the laundry room and the sewing room, which took care of the making of clothes for the children and mending when that was necessary. Children helped in all three areas, learning valuable skills for their later lives, but naturally they could not work unaided.

Jane Dixon's role as matron was delineated in the Orphanage Rules.

The duties of the Matron are:- To be responsible for the domestic arrangements of the Orphanage, to take the oversight of the instruction of the girls in domestic work, and give special attention to delicate, timid or sickly children; to have charge of all the consumable stores supplied to the Institution, also of the children's clothing, house linen, stores and furniture, and see that the same are in good order, for which, as well as for the cleanliness and sanitary condition of the Institution, she is responsible; to see that all children have a warm bath at least one evening a week; to make a daily inspection of all parts of the house, and to visit the girls dormitories before she retires to rest.

The Orphanage Rules listed several necessary staff including needlewoman, cook, laundress, and servants – but when the orphanage first opened, there was only one servant and no resident laundress. A month later, James Dixon reported to the committee that a permanent laundress was, in fact, all too necessary. Expecting washerwomen to come out to the orphanage, which was then very much in the countryside, was too much to ask and the single general servant had already given in her notice because of the pressure of the work. This situation had to be raised at two committee meetings before it was eventually agreed that Jane Dixon, in her role as matron, should be allowed to engage a new servant – and a laundress – forthwith.

James Dixon's Occurrences Book records the arrival of each member of staff, their annual holidays or sicknesses and their eventual departures. At first sight it makes disconcerting reading because the turnover of staff appears to be so frequent and so swift; many staff members stayed for only a few weeks or months, and reasons for their departures are not always given. It is likely that the orphanage could not offer very high wages but this was surely known when the staff took their positions in the first place. The orphanage opened in the August of 1891 and by Christmas, the cook and one of the 'general servants' had already left. The latter, Emily Collison, had found a job as a sewing maid in Preston but Mrs Lancaster, the cook, suffered bad health and was admitted to the Infirmary. By the time the orphanage had been open for six months, John Woods the yardsman had moved on to 'a better place' in Hellifield and Miss Ingham, who had been 'dissatisfied' first as a laundress and then as a cook, lasted a bare three months before leaving In February 1892. Was the work, or the institution itself, so awful that they could not be borne for long?

It is far more likely, when we understand that James Dixon had built the orphanage through his constant calls for funds, that he likewise made regular calls for help and many of the short-term staff were friends or church members who were volunteering to do their bit for this most worthy charitable venture. Indeed, the records do show that some temporary staff members had given their services for free or in return for simple bed and board.

Over forty years of records, thirty-one men and women worked at the orphanage for short periods ranging from a single month to one year, as sewing maids, cooks, laundresses, yardsmen and assistants. Six married couples also came to work together at the orphanage but left after a few months. The supposition that they may have offered their services out of charity is supported by the fact that a few other people are clearly noted in the records as coming to help out in times of need: Miss Mary Greaves worked as sewing maid for several brief periods over five years, Sarah Ann Hargreaves worked as laundress on a similar basis, and Mrs Lister stepped in to help in the kitchen and the sickroom, when the cook and three of the children were all ill in bed.

Reasons for leaving were not always noted in the Occurrences Book, but sometimes they were. In May 1892, Miss Read left after six weeks for a position at the YWCA in Liverpool and Sam Garlic, yardsman, left after a few weeks for a position in Clitheroe. In 1893, cook Ellen Mercer left after a month for a situation in Rochdale, and the following year Miss Bentley, cook, left after three months for a better job; likewise Mrs Walsh, who worked for four months and left for a job in Manchester. Alice Taylor worked for six months in 1905 and left to work in a shop, Elizabeth Kenyon and Cissie Harwood worked as assistants for a couple of months and then went into a cotton mill. It is to be supposed that higher wages were on offer at their new places of work.

More evidence that people came to help out of a wish to do good, rather than being truly able to do the job required of them, is apparent in several cases: Mrs Croasdale worked for a month as cook but left through ill health, Mr and Mrs Frank Carter spent three months as assistant and sewing mistress before leaving *'due to failing health'*, Mrs Harrison worked as cook for three months, leaving to go for an operation *'at the Eye Hospital'*, Mr and Mrs Hartley started as assistants but, *'not being up to the work'*, left two months later, Isabella Walsh took the post of laundress but *'could not do the work'* and so left after only a month, Mrs Elizabeth Rhodes started as sewing maid but left three weeks later *'being unable to do her work through bad health'*, and Miss Martha Ellen Worthington started work as a general assistant but left after only a month, *'not suitable for the work'*.

Only once, in forty years of records, does it seem that anyone was actually dismissed from their post. In 1902, in February, Mr and Mrs Bradley started work as assistant and sewing mistress. The following December, Mrs Bradley took to her bed and stayed there for three weeks. On her recovery, she immediately *'went to Blackburn with her husband and stayed away all afternoon without leave. They both returned to the orphanage at night about 8 o'clock.'* The very next day, they were paid up to the end of the month and left the orphanage *'by mutual arrangement, they being both altogether unsuitable for the duties required of them here.'*

Sometimes the Dixons extended the same charity to their staff as they did to their orphaned charges, even if those staff members had not been with them very long. In 1906, Mrs Platts started work as cook in the boys' orphanage and must have showed promise, as a month later she became assistant matron. She was not in good health, however, and resigned her position after eight months. However, as she was not well, she was allowed to stay at the orphanage until she recovered a full six weeks later. And in 1930, Miss May Bentley worked as assistant for just ten months and then went sick – but was not dismissed – for the next year and a half. She was accepted back into the orphanage fold, and worked for a further eight months before leaving for good.

Not all staff worked on such a temporary or short-term basis. Margaret Young, Annie Hornby and Mary Hall all worked as laundresses for over two years, Miss Anderton and Miss Gertrude Wood both worked as sewing mistresses for a year, Mrs Mary Elizabeth Clark (aged sixty-one) spent a year working as cook, Mr William Baker and Mr and Mrs Heaps worked as assistants for over two years. Miss Kenyon worked as laundress for two and a half years. In February 1903, Mary Ann Addison started work as sewing maid at the orphanage. Nearly two years later she was promoted to assistant matron. She left six months later, *'to go into a shop at Blackburn.'*

In 1892 the Misses Robinson, Sarah Jane and Grace, became permanent staff members after both had previously helped out in temporary capacities, Sarah Jane as laundress and Grace as sewing maid. Grace died the following year, but Sarah Jane remained working at the orphanage until 1894 as laundress and later, cook. Several of her friends became friends and helpers of the orphanage, notably Mrs Gaskell, who visited regularly and although never a member of staff, was often present for weeks at a time over busy periods such as Christmas and New Year.

Other, more stable, staff members included Priscilla Whalley, who started work as sewing maid and stayed for three years, leaving in June 1919. Three years after that, she returned to work as sewing maid again. Miss Gertrude Russell worked as sewing maid then laundress for four years. Miss Ethel Alderson started work as sewing maid in 1910, followed some months later by her sister Annie, who worked as laundress. Ethel stayed for three and a half years, leaving to get married in November 1913. Annie stayed until June 1915, after working as laundress and then sewing maid for four years.

Longer periods of service are recorded: Miss A Townley worked as sewing mistress for five and a half years and Ada Wood held the same post for six years. In February 1892, Fred Baxter started work as a temporary yardsman or gardener, until a permanent gardener could be found. He moved on to another job three months later, but returned to the post in June 1894 and worked as yardsman for two years before he again left to take another position. Just over a year later he returned again, and this time his wife also came to work at the orphanage, as laundress and later, sewing maid. Mr and Mrs Baxter finally moved on in February 1899, after giving seven years to the orphanage.

Miss Lucy Holden also gave seven years, starting work in 1923 as a temporary sewing maid, covering for Miss Greaves, who was sick. She returned late the following year, to take up the position permanently and was still there in 1931.

In 1907, Maggie Kenyon temporarily worked as cook for three months, and returned later that year to work as laundress, a post she held for eight years. She finally left the orphanage for good in January 1916, to get married.

Agnes McCluskie, a single girl of twenty-five, joined the staff as laundress in March 1901. Two years later she changed her position to assistant, in the boys' department of the orphanage. A year later she left, to take a position elsewhere (in Darwen) but came back eighteen months later to work as cook in the new Girls' Orphanage building.

There she stayed until the spring of 1911, when after ten years of supporting the orphanage she sailed to Canada, where she had relatives.

In 1916, Miss Marion Scott Friend started work as sewing maid, and over the next eleven years worked as dormitory maid and later cook.

Catherine Watson also supported the orphanage for eleven years, but her story was a little more remarkable. She was sixty-eight years old and a widow when she joined the staff in November 1892. She was sewing mistress for almost two and a half years before the death of her sister, in Preston, obliged her to hand in her notice. However, she remained on call, often stepping in to cover for a week or two when other staff took their holidays. She often gave her services in the sewing room and the sickroom, in return for just her board and lodgings. From 1899 she seems to have been in situ at the orphanage for three years, returning home to Preston in February 1902 when her health deteriorated, although she continued to come and stay about once a year, covering staff holidays and giving her services for free. Mrs Watson continued in her voluntary role until May 1904. She was, by this time, eighty years old.

Mrs Ellen Parkinson joined the staff in 1892 as cook. She stayed less than a year on her first term of employment, but came back two years later and was cook for the next eight years. In 1901 she was away for an extended period of sickness, staying with friends and later living in one of the almshouses, but her job was kept open for her. She died on July 14th 1912, twenty years after first accepting her post. She was clearly very close to the Dixon family; in 1909, she wrote her will, appointing James Dixon as executor and after leaving her *bed and the sheets, blankets &c belonging thereto* to her nephew, she left any money remaining in her estate to the orphanage. The resulting bequest amounted to ten pounds, one shilling and sixpence.

Mrs Annie E Wilbraham, aged forty-four and originally from Bridgnorth in Shropshire, started work as cook in 1907. She stayed for the next seventeen years, until she was sixty-one. Her daughter Violet also came to work at the orphanage, as laundress – she was certainly there in 1919 and stayed until 1924, leaving with her mother in the April of that year.

Miss Alice Wolstenholme started work as laundress in July 1915 but soon became cook and stayed for four years. After a break of five years she returned to the orphanage in 1924, working as cook for two and a half years, then becoming matron (aged forty-four), a post she held until she left the orphanage a year later, in December 1927.

Two of the longest serving staff members were Thomas Taylor and his wife, Margaret. In June, 1906, they started work as assistant and cook in the boys' building. They left nine months later. However, they came back two years later and resumed their original positions.

Five years passed, then in 1914 war broke out and Thomas was quick to step forward for his country, joining the Loyal North Lancashire Regiment. However, he barely had time to complete his basic training before the regiment was obliged to discharge him because his eyesight was less than perfect. He came back to take up his old position in January 1915.

The Taylors continued in their posts for another five years and then in March 1920, they left the orphanage. However, their time with the Dixons wasn't quite over. They returned to work as assistants less than a year later, in February 1921 and were still there nine years later. The Taylors were so well thought of that when they celebrated their Silver Wedding there was a *'merry Tea Party'* at the orphanage to mark the event. The other staff presented them with some tea knives, a pickle fork and a hand mirror. The children presented them with a fruit spoon and a brush and comb. There were games and music and it was, as James Dixon later noted, *'a most enjoyable evening'*.

In January 1929 Thomas fell ill and was taken to the Royal Infirmary, where he stayed for two weeks. He spent another month in hospital in March and in May went to a convalescent hospital in Southport, where he stayed for three weeks before coming home to the orphanage on May 23rd. All seemed well until November, when he fell ill again and three months later, in February 1930, Mr Thomas Taylor passed away. He was only fifty years old but had given the best part of twenty-four years to the orphanage. His wife, Margaret, continued to work at the orphanage until after James Dixon had finally retired and in all likelihood worked there for the rest of her life.

Challenging the Taylors for the longest service was Sydney Percy Addinall, who came to the orphanage in July 1893, aged seven. Deserted by his father, his mother went into domestic service and could not take Sydney with her. When Sydney reached working age (fourteen) James Dixon found him a job which he held for two years before moving on, presumably for better wages, but he stayed there for just a few months before moving on again. James continued to keep in touch with young Sydney, possibly because he knew that Sydney was not always entirely well. When Sydney was eighteen, James Dixon noted diplomatically in his records that 'Sydney lost his reason and was taken to Prestwich Lunatic Asylum today'. He would remain there for the next two and a half years.

When Sydney was well enough to leave the asylum, he came home to the orphanage, and three months later went to work for James Dixon's friend and committee member, Mr Airey, an art dealer. The job lasted for four months, after which he came home to live at the orphanage for a couple of months before taking another job with Captain and Mrs Ackroyd at Hazeldene, Wilpshire, his wages to be his board and lodgings and five shillings a week. Nine months later, in December 1908, he was still working for Captain Ackroyd but lodging out and earning a much better wage of sixteen shillings and sixpence a week.

At some point Sydney again returned home to the orphanage, because a diary entry in August 1913 records that 'Sydney Addinall, orphanage assistant, went for his holidays today'.

In January 1915, like so many other young men, Sydney joined the Army and James Dixon recorded his address as the Whitchurch based camp of the East Lancashire Regiment, although he was very soon transferred to the Cheshires. Poignantly, although his service records name his mother as his next of kin, his home address was noted as The Orphanage, Wilpshire. Sydney spent the rest of the war in France, although he did come home on leave at least once, staying at the orphanage for ten days. He was finally demobbed in September 1919 and came home for good.

Sydney was then given a permanent position at the orphanage, looking after the gardens and the boiler house and remained there for at least the next fifteen years. The last mention of Sydney in James Dixon's diary was of a hospital visit in July 1934, when he was forty-eight years old.

Another staff member who started her life at the orphanage as an inmate was Florrie Lenton. Florence Nightingale Lenton had been born in 1891, had lived in London and was brought to the orphanage aged seven after her father died. Her case was recommended to James Dixon by Mr Maddison of the Children's Aid Society in London, a friend and colleague of the Dixons. Over the years he was responsible for many children coming to the orphanage. Florrie's mother was a servant, out of work. Florrie did return to her mother when she turned fourteen, but came back to work at the orphanage as a sewing maid barely a month later in July of 1907. She stayed for three years, eventually going back to London to take a position there. A note in her records, two years later, says that she was now working as a lady's maid, in Farnham, Surrey.

One of the most notable members of staff was James Dixon's own daughter, Elsie Muriel. In 1915, she started work as sewing maid. She soon became assistant matron.

During the thirty-five years James Dixon was superintendent of his orphanage, around one hundred and sixty cooks, laundresses, seamstresses, yardsmen and other assistants came and went, giving their time to this worthy cause for periods varying from a week to many years. They deserve to be remembered as much as James Dixon, because without them, the orphanage would not have been able to care properly for the many hundreds of children who passed through its doors.

CHAPTER TEN

Christmas at the orphanage was a joyful time; extra efforts were made to make it so, with entreaties to local businesses for help in providing the tree, gifts and festive food. The very first orphanage Christmas, in 1891, was recorded beautifully in January's edition of *Rags and Rubies*, where James Dixon used his column *'For The Young'* to describe Father Christmas's visit. We are, of course, referring to the real Father Christmas, who visited in secret on Christmas Eve. Only James was awake when he arrived, so they had time for a long chat, which he described in detail. This is the letter he wrote to his *'Dear Young Friends'*.

Well, you know in my last letter I asked you, if you happened to come across the old gentleman, to direct him to the Orphanage, telling him there were four chimneys and plenty of room to get down.

The Orphan Boys and Girls evidently expected he would come, for they went into the fields and cut down a big Christmas tree, which was conveyed to the Orphanage and put in a big tub, and so at family worship in the School-room on Christmas Eve there stood the big bare Christmas tree, waiting for Santa Claus to come and decorate it during the night.

Well, after prayers, all went upstairs to the dormitories, and all – without exception – hung up their stockings in the most conspicuous places, to catch the eye of old Father Christmas when he arrived. Of course I hung up my stocking too. 'I don't expect to get anything in it, boys, but I just hang it up because I think it's the proper thing to encourage and keep up these old and time-honoured customs.'

So then all went to bed, and soon after eleven o'clock I peeped into the dormitories and found the thirty-seven orphans all fast asleep; and at midnight, when the Orphanage clock struck twelve, I heard a loud voice in the chimney shouting out- 'Is this the Orphanage? Is there anybody in?'

I replied, 'Aye, aye; who are you? Come in.'

'I'm Santa Claus, but I can't get down this chimney; I've got such a load of things for the Orphans, there's a big rocking horse, a box of oranges, two barrels of apples, whips and tops, toffy, nuts and sweets, bats and balls, trumpets and toys without end. How am I to get down?'

'If you can't get down the chimney, Mr. Santa Claus, please come to the front door, and I will come down and let you in.' Very soon the old gentleman was inside and busy filling the stockings with good things. When he came to a little boy's stocking, and found the following words written on a large sheet of paper near two wooden boxes, a large empty bag and two caps, old Santa Claus put his finger to his nose and laughed heartily:- 'Plese Mister Sandy Clos I has been a good boy fil all thes up plese SAMY JONES.'

Coming along to the little crib which you remember Mr. Jas. Eatough presented to the Orphanage, old Father Christmas noticed a very wee stocking hanging among a lot of others in a long row fastened to a string and near to them he read with pleasure the following lines:-

When the clock is striking twelve - When I'm fast asleep,
Down the chimney broad and black - With your pack you'll creep.
All the stockings you will see - Hanging in a row;
Mine will be the shortest one - You'll be sure to know.
Johnny wants a rocking-horse - Liza wants a dolly,
Harry wants a whip and top - He thinks dolls are folly.
As for me, my little brain - Never was the wisest;
Choose for me, old Santa Claus - What you think is nicest.

When the old man had filled all the stockings and decorated the Christmas tree, I asked him to have a cup of Fry's Cocoa with me before he left, and as he was stirring his cocoa cup I ventured to ask him who had been the good friends who had directed him to the new Orphanage.

'Oh, there was a lot of boys and girls,' he said, 'were so anxious that I should come to the Orphanage, that really I could not refuse them. There was a little boy in London-road – I don't know his name – and then there were Nellie Ritzema and her sister; also a little boy named E. L. Thacker, at Leyland, and Robert B. Smalley, at Castleton; Ethel Brewer and her brother; and then there was Bessie Horsfall (aged 12), Brian Bickerdike and his sister Mary, and Joseph Eccles and his brother Percy, besides many others whose names I don't know. But I must now be off, I have to go over to Billington, Whalley Nab, and Pendle, to fill the children's stockings there before daylight. So good-bye and God bless you,' saying which Santa Claus disappeared up the chimney.

Not long after that I went off to bed, and was just dozing into sleep, when I was suddenly awoken by a chorus of voices singing at the bedroom door, 'Christians Awake.' Getting up, I found the voices belonged to the Orphans, who had all got washed and dressed, and were enjoying the good things found in their stockings. I found a lot of good things in my stocking also, among which was a neat Christmas card, on which was written the following words:-

'From little James Prescott, to Mr Dixon, with best wishes and God's blessing this happy Christmas tide. May the Lord be unto thee an everlasting light, and thy God thy glory.'

The children named in Father Christmas's speech were just some of the *'young readers'* of *Rags and Rubies,* a few amongst the hundreds of children who read the magazine, learning in the process about the joy of giving. They responded all through the year, but naturally they were at their most generous at Christmas. The rocking horse mentioned by Father Christmas had actually been given by Ethel Brewer, whose name was so carefully included, and Bessie Horsfall (aged twelve) had sent along some tops and whips. Richard B Smalley sent a postal order for ten shillings, the result of a collection at his home where everyone, even the servants, had added to the sum. Nellie Ritzema and her sister gave ten shillings each, which they had saved up all by themselves.

In the previous edition of *Rags and Rubies,* James had described a little boy he knew who was not in the orphanage, but was very sick and very poor. He had asked the children to pray for him and some of them had gone so far as to send gifts for him and even visit, so that he also had a lovely Christmas. In this next edition, James wrote again about little Arthur, this time more poignantly.

I knew, as I told you then, that he was suffering from an incurable disease, and would not likely get better again. I told you he had a very poor home, and asked some of you to help him, which I am glad to say many of you did; and these little kindnesses on your part cheered the little boy very much. I frequently called to pray by his bedside and have a little chat with him, and he used to tell me about some of you visiting him, and bringing him nice things, and speaking kind words, for all which he seemed very thankful. Well now I have to tell you that the Lord has sent for him and little Arthur has gone to Heaven, having come through much tribulation and suffering, he has gone home to the better land. The little boy died with a prayer on his lips, fully trusting in Jesus, and although he never realised his wish to get into the Orphanage, he has now got an everlasting Home in Heaven. His spirit went to God who gave it, and his body was placed in a wee pauper's coffin and buried in the cemetery. May you and I so live as to know the joy of salvation and the glories of Heaven as this dear little boy has done.

Throughout 1892, *Rags and Rubies* carried other little anecdotes from James about the children in his care. Like any fond parent, he marvelled over their words and treasured their innocent comments and repeated them in his writings with wonderful good humour. Gathered together, these pieces serve as a charming illustration of life in the orphanage during those first few years...

The little boy you see on the picture is called Harry. He is not quite five years of age, but according to his own way of reckoning be might be far older. You will understand what I mean when I tell you that on Harry's last birthday I gave him a penny (as I gave all the orphan children on their birthday). Well, a short time after Harry came into the office and said 'Please sir, it's me birthday,' so I gave him a penny, and in a few days he came back with the same tale and got another penny, and as he was going out of the door I asked him how many 'birthdays' he had in a month, and he replied he had 'only ten.'' And when I told him he would ruin me if he went on at that speed, he only laughed, and said he was 'saving up' for a tame rabbit. Not long after that Mr. Thomas Hart called at the Orphanage, and hearing about this rabbit business he very kindly contributed a sum sufficient to buy two rabbits and a wood cot for them to live in, so I commissioned a boy in the town last week to buy two healthy rabbits, guaranteed to live five years without being sick or ill, and I have heard since that he has been on the Market making most minute inspections of the live rabbits there exposed for sale. He has made no purchase yet, being anxious to make a good bargain; but Harry and another little boy at the Orphanage named Johnny are very anxious to get this part of the business transacted.

I must now tell you about the tame rabbits the boys have got at the Orphanage. Three Rabbits were got, and their names are as follows: Ponto, Giblin, and Paganini. Ponto was given to little Johnny, Giblin to little Harry, and Paganini to little Willie. When I gave Harry his rabbit and told him it was his, and he had to look well after it, he said, 'Is it mine to keep?'

'Oh yes, it's yours to keep!'

'And is it to be mine for ever?'

'Yes, it's yours as long as ever you can keep it.'

Well, these three little boys put their rabbits in a little wood house, where they slept at night, and gambolled about in the field during the day. But one day, while the lads were playing at seesaw and the rabbits running about enjoying themselves, one of them somehow got under the plank, and was accidentally killed. The orphan boys dug a grave and reverently buried the little dead rabbit at the bottom of the Orphanage field, and the other day I noticed the boys had planted flowers on the rabbit's grave, enclosed with a stone border.

Last week a parrot was brought to the Orphanage, the kind gift of a lady. It has been hung in the dining-room, and makes a great deal of noise when the orphans come in to their meals. The boys tell me it can say 'Pretty Poll' and 'Good Night', but I can't make out what it says. Of course the boys understand parrot language better than me.

I have told my little readers before that the smallest boy in the Orphanage is called Harry, he is five years of age, and goes with the other children to the church every Sunday; he very often sits beside me in the pew, and nearly every Sunday he falls asleep during the service. Last Sunday he was fast asleep all the time the minister was preaching, so when we were walking home from church I said to the little orphan boy, who was running by my side, 'Well, Harry, what did you think of the sermon this morning?'

'It was very good,' he replied.

'What was the minister preaching about?'

'About loving Jesus.' said he.

And this is what he tells me every time I ask him after he has been asleep in church. All the sermons are the same to him, and they are all about loving Jesus.

One of the little boys at the Orphanage, who has no father or mother, came into my office the other day with a request that his money box might be opened, so that he could count his money and thus ascertain how far he had got towards raising the sum needed to buy a real live donkey, on which he had set his mind since he went with the Orphans' trip to Blackpool, where he had a donkey ride on the sands. After getting home to the Orphanage he had set about saving up for a donkey in real earnest. Well, the money box was opened, and with assistance he managed to reckon up the actual amount of his worldly possessions, which totted up to the magnificent sum of 7½d, and he had the audacity to ask me if the donkey man at Blackpool would not sell him a donkey for all this money. Fifteen ha'pennies, he said, was a lot. However, the money was returned to the box, and the wee boy made another addition to his savings that night, and went to bed to dream about donkeys.

The other day an unknown lady friend drove up to the Orphanage in a carriage and pair, and handed to the orphan boy at the gate nine tennis racquets and twelve lawn tennis balls, and, without giving any name, drove away. The orphan boys and girls have had 'rare fun' on the field with the racquets and balls on the few fine days since.

Among the many little visitors to the Orphanage during the past month were two little boys, who brought a large tame rabbit as a present to the orphan boys, and another little boy brought a little black kitten for the orphan girls. The little orphan lad I told you about last month, who was saving up for a donkey, has now got eighteen-pence, and he is getting on so rapidly with his saving, that he now says he will buy two donkeys, and give one to 'Albert.' Albert is the smallest fatherless boy who has recently been admitted to the Orphanage, and Harry and he are great friends. Some of the other boys told Harry he should buy a pony and cart with his eighteen-pence. Acting on this suggestion, he went to a farmer near and asked him the price of a horse and cart. The farmer told him that when he (the farmer) had one too many, he would give him one. And so the little lad is now wondering how long it will be, before the farmer has a pony and cart too many.

I have been thinking of the many and strange gifts that my little readers have given to the Orphanage since it was opened. The list of livestock that has been brought or sent to the Orphan Homes, include Cats, Rabbits, Pigeons, Poll-Parrot, Canary, Bullfinch, Sparrows, besides a dog and some sheep that came into the play-room of their own accord, where they had a good look round, and then went back to their own homes. But all these were last week eclipsed by the gift of a little boy who presented the orphan lads with a tame white rat. Now, this lad must have observed the words 'nothing refused,' on our Jumbles Sale bills; but really, our receiving powers must stop at rats, although this white gentleman, I am told, is a most respectable rat, and thoroughly civilized. The little boy has kindly provided it with a small house to live in. Whatever we may think about this curious gift we must give the little lad credit for the best intentions.

On Sunday afternoons the children attend service in the Orphanage school-room, to which friends are admitted. Last Sunday there was a large attendance of friends. The service was conducted by the Superintendent, and the children sang special hymns. Mr. Thomas Dawson (one of the Orphanage trustees) played the accompaniment to the hymns on the piano. The piano, I must explain, was the gift of some unknown friend. It came rolling into the Orphanage one Saturday morning, propelled by two sturdy young men, who told me they knew nothing about where it had come from nor who had given it, and professed to be in absolute ignorance of the whole affair. All I could get from them was that it was a gift from 'a friend of the orphans,' for use in the school-room and at the Sunday services. The instrument is quite new, and seems to be worth about £25. It is an excellent gift, and on behalf of the orphans I beg to thank the unknown donor, who evidently reads the begging appeals in this journal, and whose eye may perhaps catch this acknowledgment.

A very strong and influential deputation of the orphan boys have been to me with an urgent request to allow them to commence a Fife and Drum Band Fund, and they will subscribe their ha'pennies and pennies towards it. I no sooner get one thing finished than something else crops up. I blame Mr. Airey for this drum business. He very kindly comes to teach the children to sing every Thursday evening, and being a very musical man and the founder of one or two fife bands in his time, I have a very strong suspicion that the excitement among the boys over the proposed drum and fife band at the Orphanage is due in a large measure to that gentleman's suggestion. Of course he denies it, but still says it would be a capital thing, and it is quite evident I shall get no peace until it is started. The fund has therefore been commenced.

The stream of visitors to the Orphanage still continues in force. Wet or fine, in sunshine full and shower, visitors keep pouring in, and as this is likely to continue till all our friends far and near have seen through the new premises, I have stuck a notice on the front gates giving particulars of the days and times of visiting. The notice reads as follows:- 'NOTICE. The Orphanage is open to visitors from 10 a.m. to 6 p.m. on Thursdays. Persons wishing to visit the Orphanage at other times should make application in writing to the Superintendent. The children's service in the schoolroom, at half-past two on Sunday afternoons, will be open to any visitor who may wish to attend the service.'

Among the gifts presented to the Orphanage during the past month is a black and white kitten, brought by a little girl, who carried it all the way in her arms to the Orphanage door, rang the bell, and presented her gift to the attendant. The little cat seems quite at home; and the five and thirty orphan boys and girls in the Orphanage seem delighted with the latest addition to the number of inmates in the Orphanage. At present they are trying to invent a suitable name for this four-legged orphan.

A beautiful bird cage, neatly inlaid with different coloured wood, has been presented to the Orphanage; but as we have no bird to put in it, the nice cage has been laid away till we meet with some bird applying for admission. A sparrow flew in at the window the other day greatly delighting the boys, but despite the genuine welcome, he made his stay short.

As I look out of the Orphanage windows, I have also noticed Robin Redbreast at the Orphanage door on one or two of the coldest mornings lately, and yesterday a Thrush – I think it was – flew into the Dining-room when the boys were at their breakfast, but he did not stay long, for after flying through the schoolroom and along the corridors he disappeared. We had also a visit from a canary, but it came to stay, for it was a present from Masters Levi Askew and Ephraim Hindle, of Whalley New Road, who brought the little yellow bird to the Orphanage last week, where it was put into a nice cage and hung in the dining-room.

One day this month, the boys' play-room was visited by about eight or ten sheep. The Boys were at school, so the sheep had all their own way. They visited the boot-room, and after inspecting the store-cellar they *commenced to gambol about the large playroom. They had not carried on these pranks long; however, till the boys appeared on the scene and put the enemy to flight.*

A better hearted man than Mr. Airey there could not be, but I shall never forgive him for putting this Fife and Drum idea into the heads of the Orphanage boys, who are continually on to me about it, and are now agitating for permission to give an entertainment at the Orphanage in aid of the Band Fund. Several of them have given ha'pennies and pennies, and by a long pull, a strong pull, and a pull altogether, they think the £5 might be raised to buy second-hand instruments to commence the Fife and Drum Band at the Orphanage.

Judging from these vignettes, life in the orphanage was, for these children, a happy and fulfilling experience. They were encouraged to be children, to play, to have dreams and work towards making them realities. Their surrogate parents, James and Jane, were warm and friendly supporters as well as guardians and caregivers, helping the children to be the best possible people they could be. This was not institutional life as it was commonly known and it bore no relation at all to the dreaded workhouse; it was as close to a privileged home-life as it could possibly be. There is no doubt that the children appreciated all the advantages they were offered by their loving guardians.

Incidentally, readers will be pleased to know that the little boys did eventually raise enough money to pay for the instruments needed for a proper fife and drum band. They practised diligently and were soon giving performances to raise funds for their home, the orphanage.

CHAPTER ELEVEN

Two years after the orphanage building opened, James Dixon was pushing for a new fund to be started, to provide another building of the same size and extent, for girls. It had always been understood that housing both boys and girls under the same roof was not really suitable. James also wanted to build a workshop for the boys and a small hospital – there was plenty of available land, but no money. The committee agreed and James started the new fund with £10 from his personal account. It would be several years before this new plan came to fruition, but the commencement of a new fund helped to solidify the intention.

The need for a new building and therefore more bed space was emphasised by the facts and figures in the orphanage's Annual Reports; in 1893 the report stated that the committee had received forty-six applications for admission, of which only eleven had been accepted, the main reason being lack of space. The report was also keen to describe the activities of the children, from their schoolwork to their practical achievements.

All the children attended Salesbury School, but they were also expected to help with chores in the orphanage, and the girls also worked in the sewing room, learning valuable skills and also producing useful garments. In 1893 the report carried a list of these articles, produced since the orphanage had begun:

6 frocks, 17 aprons, 6 chemises, 20 pairs of stockings, 24 stockings refooted, 8 shirts, 24 handkerchiefs, 7 mittens and cuffs, 5 bags, 6 tea-cloths, 10 iron-holders, 50 floor-cloths, 5 pillow-slips, 8 night shirts, 15 garters.

In November 1893, a daughter was born into this enormous orphanage family. She was to be the first of three daughters born to the Dixons and raised in the orphanage, and the Dixons named her Isabella. It must have been fun for the children to have a baby in their midst and as Isabella grew up she would certainly never lack playmates. But less than a year after the orphanage celebrated its first birth, it suffered its first death.

It was inevitable that in such a large 'family', children would become sick and some would have accidents requiring medical treatment. This caused extra strain on the orphanage's slim funds, because medical treatment was not free, as it is today. Dr Pollard, a trustee of the orphanage, did visit the orphanage to attend to common ailments and gave his services free but for more serious illnesses James was obliged to beg for 'hospital tickets' from the public, to pay for hospital visits.

This was an age when common childhood illnesses were much more dangerous than they are today and outbreaks of measles and scarlet fever were to be expected. Tuberculosis was common, typhoid was not unheard of. To nurse one child through a childhood infection is worrying and time-consuming enough for most parents but, in an institution containing dozens of children, these outbreaks sometimes meant that the sickroom was home to six or seven children at a time, for a period of several days. These childhood diseases occasionally led to other medical problems but with Dr Pollard calling daily, the children were in safe and knowledgeable hands. Only scarlet fever necessitated the removal of a child to the Fever Hospital, as it was judged to be such a serious and infectious disease that the sufferer should be kept in isolation.

The orphanage suffered remarkably few deaths during all of its long existence but arguably the most poignant must be the demise of little Alice Tattersall in August 1894, the first death to be recorded. Along with her older brother, she had been admitted to the orphanage six months after it opened, as both children were 'motherless, homeless and in great moral peril...' Alice was eight years old at the time and it was soon observed that she was much less strong than her brother. It was suspected that she may have inherited a weak and 'consumptive' constitution from her mother who had died a few years before. Because she was so sickly, she was a solitary child, rarely playing outside with the other children. Both staff and children treated her gently and referred to her as their *'Little Pet Lamb'*.

Two and a half years after coming into the orphanage, Alice came home from school one day complaining that she had a headache and felt sick. She was put to bed, but did not feel better the next day and the day after that was so much worse that the doctor was summoned. By next morning, Alice had sunk into unconsciousness and Dr Pollard was forced to admit that there was little hope for her recovery. Two days later, early in the morning, Alice Tattersall died. The cause of her death was diagnosed as tubercular meningitis. She was just nine years old.

Alice was buried in Salesbury churchyard, in a grave quickly provided for the orphanage by the Rev. P H Hart, at no charge. Recording the event in his diary, James commented that the grave was dug very deep, for it was only to be expected that other young souls might someday be buried there also. In fact, the orphanage would suffer a remarkably low death rate, but even so, in 1919 the vicar of Salesbury Church donated one more grave space for the orphanage's use.

James described Alice's funeral as *'...a very touching sight. There was no hearse and no mourning coaches, but the little coffin was borne to the churchyard by eight of the orphan boys who acted as pallbearers; the girls marched in front, and the little boys behind, each child carrying a flower. The funeral procession was met at the churchyard gates by the Rev. P. Hopwood Hart and the Rev. George Hart, who conducted the funeral service, after the orphans sang a suitable hymn around the open grave.'*

Two months later, James suffered a more personal loss. His dear father, James Dixon senior, fell ill early in October and, when he had not recovered three weeks later, James took time to go and visit him in his home in Eaglesfield, Scotland. He found his father very ill indeed and unable to eat. He died just a week later, aged seventy-nine, and James was charged with organising a *'very respectable'* funeral in his home village.

Christmas followed close behind this sadness, but as far as the orphanage children were concerned, it was simply a time for fun and celebration. On Boxing Day 1894, a good dinner of roast beef and plum pudding was served to over sixty boys and girls, the number swelled by the inclusion of some past scholars who were keen to revisit their former home and their surrogate parents. In the evening there was a concert and finally, the enormous Christmas tree was divested of its load of presents. There was a small gift for every child. Next day there was a special treat for the children of coffee, buns and fruit, generously given by one Mr William Dewhurst, and two days later other friends of the orphanage came to entertain them with a magic lantern show.

Once the festivities were over, sadness followed once again when, on New Year's Eve, Jane Dixon's mother died at her home in Blackburn. This must have been a difficult time for Jane; she was expecting her second child at the time which must have added a particular poignancy to her grief, but it is to be hoped that she was helped by the distraction of organising New Year's Eve celebrations in the orphanage for the children to enjoy. The next day, all the children were treated to a *'tea party and entertainment'* at Salesbury School and three days later, on January 4th, Jane's mother was buried at Blackburn cemetery. The year had ended in a mixture of joy and sadness, but the New Year, 1895, would be busier than ever. The Dixons' second daughter, Elsie Muriel, arrived on March 19th at 10 o'clock in the morning.

As well as looking after his own growing family and dealing with daily orphanage business, James and the committee were also planning to extend the orphanage building. It had always been the intention to invest in a second building, but as funds were always short, an interim plan was decided upon: to extend the east end of the current building, thereby providing ten more beds for needy children.

In January 1895, the committee decided to transfer the residue of money still left in the original Building Fund to a new Extension Fund. Progress was remarkably swift – plans for the extension were drawn up and, by May, Messrs Briggs & Wolstenholme were engaged as architects. On August 31st the foundation stone was laid with all due ceremony. It is no surprise to learn, from the minutes, that James Dixon had managed to persuade the committee to agree to extra building work, so that both the east and west sides of the building were extended at the same time. This would provide another twenty beds for needy children, instead of the expected ten.

During the months of planning, a small incident is described in the Occurrences Book that illuminates the growing need for an entirely separate building so that boys and girls could live in separate accommodation.

This evening soon after the children went to bed about 9.30 one of the boys came downstairs and informed the Matron (Mrs Dixon) that two boys were running along the corridor towards the Girls' end. Mrs Dixon went upstairs and on seeing her, the two boys ran into the sickroom and hid under a bed. Two very little boys and three elder girls to look after them sleep in the sickroom and have done for some weeks. The Superintendent (Mr Dixon) was sent for and he severely reprimanded the boys. The Matron similarly punished the 3 girls for disobeying orders in not having the sickroom door locked according to instructions.

In those Victorian days, the practice of housing boys and girls under one roof was a very real moral issue in the eyes of both the church and the general public, whose support, both emotional and financial, was of utmost importance. It must surely have been of great concern to James Dixon and his wife and the rest of the trustees but, whilst James may already have had ambitions of building a separate orphanage building to house only girls, it would be five more years before that idea was realised.

In the meantime, deserving children continued to arrive at the doors of the orphanage with great regularity and so the extension plan was a necessary stopgap. One of the most ambitious fund-raising efforts was *'Pound Day'*, which happened on June 24th 1895. Supporters and friends were asked to give either a pound in money or a pound in weight of something else: foodstuffs, candles or anything which would be useful to the orphanage. Thus the less well-off could give a pound of vegetables at little cost and still feel they were doing something worthwhile. It was a clever idea, which became a successful annual event. In 1895, over four hundred individual gifts were received, amounting to £86 13s 10d in cash, and gifts in kind worth over £42.

Children continued to arrive, grow up and move out to take up employment, but still the need remained for a separate building for girls. Fund-raising was stepped up to cover the ever increasing costs of caring for a rapidly growing family of more than fifty children. The monthly fundraiser magazine *Rags and Rubies* carried repeated pleas for donations, in cash or in kind. Every issue included comprehensive lists of everyone who had donated, from the largest bequest from a wealthy patron's will, right down to the smallest amount raised by a classroom of children from the proceeds of a concert they had given.

However, more definite and predictable means of funding needed to be found and one way of doing this was through an endowment scheme. A single donation of £500, when invested, would provide enough annual revenue to cover the cost of keeping one child in the orphanage. The giver would be said to be sponsoring a cot and a brass plaque, duly inscribed with their name, would be mounted above one of the children's beds. The scheme resulted in many brass plaques being engraved over the years and they still survive at the orphanage building. Many of the names will be instantly recognisable to history-minded Blackburn residents; Elma Yerburgh and Daniel Thwaites are just two of the familiar names.

On August 19th 1896, the newly extended building was formally opened. The new parts of the building housed twenty beds, a new kitchen and larder, a sickroom and a playroom. Mrs J W Clayton, strong supporter of the orphanage, undertook the formality of opening the building and was presented with a silver key by Mr Brierley and a bouquet by one of the orphanage girls.

The 1896 Annual Report carried a description of the ceremony and explained the continuing need for the extension, from the point of view of the committee. In the previous year there had been forty-three applications to the orphanage. Only eight of these children had been admitted, because of the lack of room.

It is a good work to take up the cause of those little ones whose earliest days have been spent in comparative discomfort, and who have been suddenly brought face to face with destitution through the failure of means or the death of the bread-winner. For instance, it must be hard to refuse the admission of little Frank, the son of a deceased overlooker, with nine brothers and sisters equally unprovided for; or Albert, whose grandmother is responsible for the maintenance of six hungry little people; or Minnie, whose mother has five to keep and clothe; or Alice, who has no relations living; or Fred, whose aunt is burdened with four additional children to feed since death called the father away and the cruel hand of insanity was laid upon the mother; or Willie, the son of a weaver who left eight fatherless and motherless children.

If further evidence was really needed of the valuable work being done at the orphanage, the same report printed some letters from children who had left the orphanage, after reaching working age and being found jobs. Here is one example, from a girl then living in Scotland.

I am coming over to England for a week at Christmas, when I shall spend a few days with you at the Orphanage. I would like to be in England a day or two before Christmas, so that I could be at the Orphanage on Christmas Day. Will the other girls be there as usual? I would like to see them all again. I often wish I could come back to stay for ever. I was dreaming one night that we had come back to stay for ever, but I was sorry when I woke up to find it was only a dream.

One child had recently been 'home' to the orphanage for a holiday and her mistress had written: '*I was glad for her to come to the Orphanage, and fully appreciate your kindness in having her for the week. She thinks there is no place like the Orphanage.*'

In May 1897, the orphanage mourned the death of Miss Nancy Derbyshire, who had always been such a good friend to them. James and many of the children attended her funeral, where the children sang a hymn and placed flowers on the grave. It was remembered that

106

Miss Derbyshire had paid for the land on which the orphanage was built, had performed the opening ceremony and had then made an annual subscription of £25 to the Maintenance Fund. In the previous year she had donated enough money to endow two cots, which were named for herself and her sister, Mrs Sames. The account published in the Annual Report for that year described her as *'a true philanthropist, and her passing away removes from among us one of the most genial and kind-hearted of women.'*

In April 1898, almost a year after Miss Derbyshire had passed away, James Dixon received a little note from a James Hargreaves. It said: *'Dear Mr Dixon, The enclosed was found attached to the Coal Case at the time of Miss Derbyshire's death and I think you ought to have and preserve it. Yours truly, James Hargreaves.'*

Miss Derbyshire's note read: *'I give this coal cabinet to the Orphanage, Wilpshire. I think it would be useful in the sickroom. Nancy Derbyshire. March 29, 1894.'*

Written so long before her death, this was a touching addendum to the lady's support of the orphanage. The note was indeed kept and preserved, carefully paper-clipped onto a page in the Minute Book.

The work Miss Derbyshire had so long supported continued. It was in the year of her death that work on the new Ragged School in Bent Street finally began, with James Dixon and Mr Walkden laying the founders' stones on July 3rd. The new building would be opened just over a year later, in October 1898. The orphanage magazines and annual reports carried many stories of children who had now grown up and been placed in jobs, both in Blackburn and around the country. The child who did not take best advantage of the opportunity availed to them by the orphanage was rare indeed and James made a strong case for the value of the work being done both by the Ragged School and the orphanage.

Suppose the orphanage had never existed, the fatherless children who have been admitted might have been like many others who are today through no fault of their own, but for the want of a good start in life recruiting the ranks of the unemployed, drifting into crime or vagrancy and filling our jails and workhouses, where they have to be kept at a great cost to the country. It is a well-known fact that from £35 to £40 a year is the sum required to maintain a criminal in prison, and be it remembered that for the same amount we can maintain three orphans in our Home where they are clothed, fed, educated, and finally placed in some position from which to start the ascent of the social ladder, and lead honest reputable lives.

Sending the children out into the world was, however, a slow process, as they must attain the age of fourteen before they would be found work and lodgings and stand on their own two feet in the world. A concert given in the town hall in January 1898 – seven years after the orphanage opened – included performances by some of the children who had been the first to be admitted in 1891, including Andrew Killeen, Eliza Urmston and Rachel Taylor. The concert included songs, pieces from the Ragged School Prize Brass Band, recitations and demonstrations of dumb-bell and Indian club exercises taught by one Grace Blacklock. The concert was repeated at Withnell a month later and both events were successes, both in the way they were received and the money they raised.

It was also in this year that James Dixon's third daughter, Gertrude, was born. His personal family was complete but his adopted family continued to grow. Indeed, by November of 1898, Salesbury Day School was obliged to enlarge its premises, which had for some time not really been sufficient for the needs of the local children and the growing number of orphanage children, which had increased by now to seventy-one. The Rev. Hart wrote to James and the committee pointing out that the orphanage should take at least some responsibility for the cost of this work and asked for a contribution of £50. It was hard to find an argument against this logic, despite the fact that any available money could easily be spent in other ways more immediately beneficial to the orphanage. It took a year, but the sum of £50 was eventually collected from a variety of subscribers and from the proceeds of a concert given especially for the purpose and was handed over to the school.

The sheer number of children had also overwhelmed the Wesleyan Chapel, where the children attended a service on Sunday evenings. The minister was obliged to write with the suggestion that they attend the morning service instead, when there was more room in the Chapel. Fortunately the wardens of Salesbury Parish Church had no objection to the children attending the evening service, and so the order was reversed.

Yet despite the growing number of children, life in the orphanage was calm, structured, and happy. A visitor, who travelled from Clitheroe in May 1898 to attend the Sunday afternoon service, wrote an article describing the place and the children.

Some forty boys, neatly dressed, were walking in processional order parading the grounds by a circular march. We were much surprised to notice the regularity of their steps and the excellence of their conduct, notwithstanding that there was no visible commander.

He described how after the service, each child shook his hand before leaving and then they all went outside to play or walk in the grounds.

Mr Dixon in the meantime escorted us through the building, which for its sanitary arrangements, cleanliness, and homelike comforts is most admirable, and our interest in the place was intensified by Mr Dixon giving us a brief history of the Institution.

A gabbling parrot, which whistled like a steam engine, was caged in the dining-hall, and was one of the numerous gifts last 'Pound Day.' Over the mantel-piece in the kitchen the words 'Waste not, want not' are chiselled upon a waving ribbon. Very appropriate words indeed, not only for the guidance of those in the culinary department, but in every other station of life.

We were not a little amused at a scene wrought in iron, which hangs above the mantel of the back parlour, which is an almost animated picture of an old-time doctor extracting a tooth with a large pair of pincers. The patient is evidently writhing in direst agony, whilst to gain leverage the doctor has one foot on the patient's chest, and with both hands is tearing the ugly offender out, whilst the expression on the face of the patient is woeful, awful indeed.

The delightful impressions derived from our visit will remain as a green and fertile spot within the memory for many years.

In 1900, James wrote in the Annual Report that he had heard from Peter Tomlinson, the little boy who was mentioned in his diary all those years ago and whose discovery was a pivotal moment in James's decision to devote his life to work with children. It had been ten years since he found little Peter, half-naked, barefoot and hungry, sleeping on straw in a slum-house in Copy Nook. Peter was now a navy boy and had recently written from the ship Caledonia, which was currently at South Queensferry, near Edinburgh.

I write these few lines hoping to find you and Mrs Dixon and all the children in the Orphanage in good health, as it leaves me at present. Dear Sir, I am getting on very well; you know I was working at the bleach works, and they began to run short time, so I joined the Navy to make a man of myself. I have not got a black mark yet, and I mean to keep it so. I was confirmed last Friday by the Bishop of Edinburgh. The chaplain of the ship is very kind to us. I will be over on furlough at Christmas, and I will be sure to come and see you.

A more touching letter was featured in the 1901 Annual Report, from Ernest Stevenson, who had been brought to the orphanage when his parents died and was now running his own successful business. He had clearly been deeply affected by his experiences and, not only appreciated the opportunity he had been given by James Dixon, but also felt deeply for children he saw daily who were in the same situation from which he had been rescued.

Dear Mr Dixon, I received your kind invitation to the Annual Reunion of scholars past and present. I heartily thank you, though I am very sorry to say I cannot take advantage of it, much as I would like to, for, as you know, Saturday is the busiest day of the week for anyone in business like myself – just the day I could not come, for (I am pleased to say) I have started in business for myself, and have been here six weeks, after having managed a large hair-dressing establishment for over two years. I am pleased to say I have got along very nicely ever since I left the Orphanage, but I always look back with fond thoughts of the time I spent under your kind parental care, and think of those deep truths that made such a lasting impression on our then childish minds; indeed, during my few years' residence in Manchester, I have painfully observed the slumdom, misery, poverty and wretchedness that seem inseparable from modern city life, and I have been very forcibly struck as to the necessary existence of such Institutions as the Orphanage. How I have contrasted the dirty little ragged children in the slums (little diamonds in the rough, some of them are) with the bright, clean, and happy-faced darlings in such places as yours, and I often thought of the romps in the meadow and the picnics we had as children at Wilpshire, and the kindness bestowed on us. Oh, how I wish and pray for success in your kind endeavours to brighten and make happy the lives of children that might otherwise be ill-spent and wretched. I will conclude with fond love and best wishes to all. Believe me to be, Yours very sincerely, Ernest Stevenson.

This report continued with updates about other children who were now out in the world and doing well, with excerpts from their letters and those of their employers. But sadly James also had to report a death, that of a little boy called Frank Green, who had been ill for some time with a diagnosis of 'Tubercular Meningitis' and had died in March. He had been admitted to the orphanage only fifteen months previously and was the baby of the family, only five years old when he died.

Frankie was not a healthy child; he had frequent fits and had he not died, the tuberculosis which killed him would certainly have seriously affected his future quality of life, as there was no easy complete cure. During the last five weeks of his illness, staff had taken turns sitting through the night with him, and Dr Pollard and his son, also now a doctor, had visited every day. Everything that could be done for him was done.

Frank was only the second child to die at the orphanage in ten years, which is a fact worthy of note. His funeral took place on March 11th, a short service being conducted in front of the orphanage by James Dixon, before the coffin was carried to the graveyard by eight boys, for a more formal ceremony and burial in the same plot as Alice Tattersall. Even the lettering on the tombstone was engraved by an old orphanage boy, who was now apprenticed to a stonemason. Underneath the children's names, the dedication read, *'Jesus called a little child unto him; For of such is the kingdom of Heaven.'*

On a different subject altogether, the 1901 report also described the food used by the orphanage in that year – ten thousand 2lb loaves, 8,700 quarts of new milk, over a ton of sugar and more than half a ton of butter. This list was followed by the statement *'There is no waste, no want and no extravagance.'*

1902 saw the loss of two remarkable men in the history of the orphanage: John Thomas Walkden, and Joseph Brierley. Walkden had resigned from the orphanage committee a few years previously, concentrating all his efforts on the Ragged School from then on, and he would be greatly missed. Joseph Brierley had been not only a member of the orphanage committee, but had contributed to the funds very generously and repeatedly. His death was marked with an obituary in the orphanage magazine and Annual Report, with an account of his funeral at which a dozen orphanage boys had, at his request, sung his favourite hymn at the graveside.

The Annual Report also included the usual selection of letters from old boys and girls, including one from Andrew Killeen, one of the first children to enter the orphanage on the day it opened. He was currently working in Belgium and although he would later settle happily and even marry a local girl, his first letter gave away his initial homesickness. *'I don't like it here, it is too fast for me altogether; but I don't want to leave until I have another place to go to. I should like to say here, sir, that I spent the happiest days of my life in the Orphanage.'*

More importantly, 1902 was the year in which a major decision was taken: finally to build the new orphanage building. The previous year had seen a doubling in the number of applications and it was felt that there was little choice but to invest in a new building, the same size as the first, doubling the number of available beds. A new drive began to raise funds and, because the need was seen to be so great, it was agreed that any shortfall could be borrowed from the Endowment Fund, to be repaid over time.

Two years of hard fund-raising followed and, in August of 1904, the foundations of the girls' building were dug and building commenced. The new project was marked with the usual ceremonial laying of a foundation stone – or rather, two stones. One was laid by James Dixon and bore the date 1904, whilst the other bore the initials LCKW and was laid, in an appropriately touching fashion, by a three-year-old boy: Master Leonard Cresswell King-Wilkinson, youngest son of a prominent local lawyer. These stones can still be seen, to the left and right of the main entrance of the existing orphanage building in Wilpshire.

The Blackburn Times covered the ceremony and commented particularly about young Leonard.

...a handsome little boy of just three short years, whose brown soft hair fell in a straight fringe across his white forehead, and on whose baby face was a look of calm expectancy. Held in his father's arms, a picture of sweet childish fairness in his dainty white coat and dress edged with fine filmy embroidery, little Master Leonard Cresswell King-Wilkinson was the object on which all eyes were fixed.

The exquisite ceremony over, the child turned to his mother and smiled; the crowd beamed with delight. Mr Gregson, the photographer, busy with his camera, made preparations to take some record of the scene, and when at last he smilingly gave the signal and made the exposure, the sun shot through the lens, and kissing the dark negative within, left on it the impression of Master Leonard King-Wilkinson standing on the stone, his mother on his right hand and his father on his left.

Around two thousand people attended the ceremony. They then had permission to tour the existing thirteen-year-old building, which they did with great interest, inspecting the neat dormitories, the sickroom (which was reassuringly empty), the dining room and sewing room, the kitchen, bathroom, storeroom and laundry. The newspaper report spoke glowingly of the boys' reading-room and its wall, which was papered with a lacquered collage of pictures, making the room a pleasant retreat.

It was here that one of the orphans drew his clever pencil sketches, evidence of a talent which gained him free admission to the Blackburn Technical School, where last week he passed first class in freehand, first class in model drawing, and first class in drawing on the blackboard. And yet 8 years ago the boy, without father and mother, wandered, clothed in rags, a vagrant through the streets.

Mr. Dixon shows the drawings with infinite pride, and one wonders as one gazes at them how many embryo painters, sculptors, inventors, politicians, or even leaders of armies, this great building shelters when night falls like a curtain and the lights are put out; how many ornaments to their country this good man and his wife are rearing; how many distinguished intellects this corner of Lancashire is preserving and developing to add to the brilliance of the nation.

In the corridor a little girl of about five or six, catching sight of Mr Dixon, runs up to him smiling, and lovingly clasps his hand, dancing along beside him wherever he goes. She has no father, only a widowed mother left with a large family to support, but as she looks up laughing into Mr Dixon's face one sees that the mite has found someone who stands in the place of the parent she has lost.

When the new Girls' Orphanage building opened some months later, the extra places it provided were quickly filled and the two buildings now housed a total of a hundred and two children. The constant struggle to raise funds continued; seven beds had now been endowed (the lump sums given for this purpose invested and the interest being enough to maintain one child) but this still left dozens unsupported. A new fund had been started – the Children's Cot Fund – whereby local children were encouraged to donate shillings towards the endowment of a cot. As ten thousand shillings were needed to make up the required £500, the effort could take some years but, by 1904, one thousand shillings had already been gratefully received.

In 1904 around twenty children were placed out in jobs, and this was an additional expense as they were all given outfits of clothing and necessary personal articles for their new lives, which cost a total of four or five pounds.

A boy's outfit comprised *'two suits of Clothes, two Caps, one Necktie, two Collars, four Handkerchiefs, two Day Shirts, two Night Shirts, one pair of Braces, two pairs of Stockings, two pairs of Boots, one pair of Slippers, one Hair Brush, one Dressing Comb, one Bible, one Tin Box'.*

A girl's outfit comprised *'one Jacket or Cape, two Trimmed Hats, two Dresses, two Upper Skirts, two Flannel Petticoats, one pair of Stays, two Chemises, two pairs of Drawers, two Night Dresses, four Handkerchiefs, two Bags, two pairs of Stockings, one pair of Gloves, two pairs of Boots, one pair of Slippers, one Hair Brush, one Dressing Comb, one Umbrella, one Bible, one Tin Box'.*

Fortunately, by 1904 there was a source of funding especially for this purpose, the Thomas Porter Equipment Fund, which gave the orphanage a grant of around £30 annually.

The new building, the Girls' Orphanage, was formally opened by Miss Baynes, of Salmesbury Old Hall, on July 27th 1905. The total cost, as would be expected, had risen from the original estimate of £5,000 to £6,600, and despite urgent appeals for help, £4,300 of this remained to be settled. Donations continued to arrive, but there were a number of different funds connected with the orphanage and James Dixon and the rest of the committee were diligent about allocating money to the purpose for which it was intended. For example, just as the building was opened, a telegram had arrived from a solicitor, announcing the death of Mr Aspinall Clayton and his bequest of £1,000 to be used to endow two cots. Despite the heavy debt, the money was indeed used to endow the cots.

The debt continued to reduce uncomfortably slowly until, a year later, the committee received another bequest, from the estate of the recently deceased William Bashall Park, of Ollerton Hall in Withnell. The legacy amounted to £2,000 and thankfully, no special condition was applied to the money, so it was with a sense of great relief that it was applied to the building debt, halving it in one sweep to just £2,000.

By now it will be clear that the lack of money had never held James Dixon back when he wanted to instigate a new project. In the same way, when there was a little money to spare, he was always ready with a suggestion about how it could best be put to good use. In 1906 he approached Mr Hindle, of the Ragged School, with a new plan. There was, for once, a little money in the bank which was not required for any immediate purpose and James had long seen the need for some more dedicated work amongst disabled children. There had always been a *'Cripple Committee'* as part of the Ragged School work, which from 1898, had visited such children in their homes with gifts of fruit, toys and books, and had helped provide such necessary items as crutches and wheelchairs and taken them for days out in the summer months. In 1898 there were just seventeen children on their visiting list but, by 1903, there were a hundred and twenty and, as the numbers grew, it became apparent that some of the children needed more than just day trips and home visits.

In 1907, with James's encouragement, a house in Heys Lane at Livesey was rented for five years and used as a full-scale convalescent and respite home for crippled children. The house was actually a former pub, 'The Farmer's Boy', which naturally required some alterations but in other ways was eminently suitable as it had plenty of room and was in a healthy countryside area. The home was officially opened on June 17th by the mayoress, Mrs F T Thomas, amidst the usual ceremonial atmosphere. It was able to provide respite for children and their families for periods varying from a fortnight to twelve weeks. This gave the workers the opportunity to provide more definite medical treatment and subsequent convalescence for those children who were so badly in need.

Meanwhile at the orphanage, the annual reports of 1908 and onwards were able to announce several more endowments; in 1908 the *'Dorothy Margaret Cot'* was endowed by Mrs Baynes of Samlesbury Old Hall to commemorate the wedding of her daughter who had opened the new Girls' Building three years previously; the *'James Hoyle Cot'* was endowed by Alderman James Hoyle, who had already endowed one cot in memory of his late wife; and Mr George Riley of Rishton endowed a cot which would bear his own name. In 1909 the collection of ten thousand shillings by local children finally reached its target and the *'Children's Cot'* was able to be fully endowed – but the drive was immediately replaced by a new one, for children to raise enough on a yearly basis to support two, or even more, cots. In 1912, James Wilcock JP, who had been a trustee of the orphanage, died and left a bequest of £2,000 for the endowment of two beds in each of the boys' and girls' buildings. He had already endowed one bed at the orphanage and made a donation of another £500.

In 1912 there was a grand celebration. It was twenty-one years since the opening of the first orphanage building and, on July 23rd, the whole day was given over to fun. James Dixon recorded it in his diary.

21st anniversary and the event was celebrated all day. There was a substantial lunch, and several old boys and girls came for afternoon tea and played games in the grounds. Union Jack was hoisted on the flag pole. Prizes were given for the children's garden plots; the best and the neatest. In the evening gramophone records were played, and everyone joined in singing the song 'A Happy Family We'. Three cheers were given for the many friends who had helped the Orphanage over the years, and the evening ended with a hymn and evening prayers.

The Annual Report in 1912 carried a description of a visit in September by a group from Chorley's Eaves Lane Congregational School, whom James had often addressed. The visitors talked especially about the homely atmosphere of the orphanage.

Some were conducted over the large buildings, and were delighted to find everything so clean and orderly; the equipment being perfect. Others of the party had conversations with one or another of the inmates, and it was obvious that the affection bestowed upon the little ones by 'Father' (as Mr Dixon is tenderly called) is reciprocated. It was touching to see how lovingly they looked up to him as they ran to take him by the hand whilst he was passing through their department.

One little group was sad, and evidently had touched the hearts of some of the matrons of the party, as they had found the cause of sorrow. It was because they were to leave Mr Dixon's hospitable roof in a few days. In another room, one of the nurses was petting and mothering a sweet little tot which had not been well for a few days. A princess could not have experienced more kindness or attention than did this little fatherless child.

1913 was a less happy year; the orphanage was afflicted with an outbreak of measles, which was swiftly followed by scarlet fever, the afflicted boys being moved to the Fever Hospital where they would be isolated. Scarlet fever was notoriously infectious; the orphanage was thoroughly disinfected from top to bottom to prevent the outbreak taking a real hold. Sadly, one of the boys in the Fever Hospital, Thomas Brunskill, died there. He was ten years old. The Salesbury Parish Church magazine recorded the event.

On February 7th the funeral took place of the late Thomas Brunskill, formerly of the Orphanage, and one of the scholars at our School. His death occurred at the Fever Hospital, to which he had been removed while suffering from Scarlet fever. He was a well-conducted little lad, and much liked by his companions and teachers. Both they and Mr and Mrs Dixon feel his loss, and we take this opportunity of expressing our sympathy with them. The Orphanage children were present at the funeral, and sang the hymn 'Nearer, My God, To Thee,' at the graveside.

Deaths at the orphanage had been remarkably infrequent. However, more deaths would be reported during the next few years, not from poverty or illness but from the inhumanities of warfare, as the Great War exploded into Europe.

CHAPTER TWELVE

As World War I erupted, the 1914 Annual Report naturally commented on it, referring to *'the trying time we have had financially during the last quarter of the past year, caused by the terrible European war now raging'* and the fact that the orphanage was *'worthily represented'* in the Forces, as over thirty old boys had already left their jobs to join up. Before the war was over, well over a hundred boys would have served in the army and navy and ten would lose their lives. The first of the dead, Alfred Burns, had already fallen by the time the Annual Report was published.

Alfred had been one of the first boys to be admitted to the orphanage. With his brother, Emanuel, he had moved there from the Boys' Rest when the orphanage opened in 1891. He was eight, his brother eleven. Less than two years later, the boys' mother was in a position to reclaim her sons and support them and this she did, taking Emanuel home in the April of 1893, and Alfred in the August. Yet, despite the brevity of their stay at the orphanage, the boys kept in touch.

Alfred's mother died in 1902, when Alfred was twenty-two, and he decided to join the army. He was thirty-four when World War I broke out. His regiment was immediately sent to France, where he served all too briefly before losing his life, in December 1914.

Another orphanage casualty was Charlie Gray, who was wounded in France in the first few months of the war but, thankfully, recovered. He had come into the orphanage in 1905 as a twelve-year-old, after both his parents had died and his grandmother, who had taken care of him for three years, could no longer afford to keep him. He returned to live with his grandmother as soon as he was of working age and could contribute to the household, enlisting three years later, in 1910. He served in India and Africa and in 1914 his regiment was sent to France. He suffered gunshot wounds in his arm and his leg, lost two fingers and was sent to a French hospital, then to hospital in London, and finally Preston Barracks, although it was not until the following April that he was recovered enough to visit his old family at the orphanage. Charlie eventually emigrated to Australia and it is testament to the fondness he felt for his time at the orphanage that when he came back to England for a visit many years later, in 1933, he made sure he called at his old home.

Another visitor to the orphanage in 1914 was Andrew Killeen, who had been in the orphanage since its opening in 1891. He was eight years old at the time and had spent four months in hospital, but his parents were nowhere to be found. So, when he was discharged, he came to the orphanage. When he grew up and left for work, he found a job as a groom and in 1902 was offered a job in Belgium, working for nobility – truly a 'rags to riches' tale. A year later he was working for a horse trainer in Chantilly, France, and some months after that, moved back to stables in Belgium. He visited the orphanage at Christmas 1905 and James Dixon reported in his records that Andrew was *very well and doing well*. His next visit, in 1914, was under very different circumstances; along with his wife and two small sons, he had been forced to flee to England because of the war in their homeland. He did return to Belgium when the war was over and continued to keep in touch with James Dixon.

Throughout the war, the Annual Reports included letters from old boys serving abroad, often in response to letters first sent by James Dixon, enquiring after their welfare. Percy Conway wrote from the HMS *Emperor of India*.

You will please excuse me for not writing before, but we have been at sea for some time and I could not write sooner. I thank you very much for the parcel of good things you sent me. I think it is very good of you looking up your old boys like that. I must say you have got a good few at the front. I have never heard anything of Harry Parker yet. Perhaps he is in another depot. I am quite well myself, and hope everyone at Wilpshire Orphanage is the same.

Percy had spent virtually his whole childhood in the orphanage, admitted when he was just five years old, in 1903. He left in 1911 and spent a couple of years working in shops and on farms before joining the navy in 1913, aged seventeen. By 1917 he was signalman on a mine sweeper, the *Godetia*, and happily he survived the war unscathed.

Other letters, without the authors' names, appeared in the 1914 Annual Report. They were all cheerful letters, from boys who felt, as did their compatriots, that the war would soon be over.

Please accept my sincere thanks for your kindness to me in sending me a parcel. I am extremely proud to be able to count you amongst my friends. Allow me to say that your gift arrived in time for Christmas Day. We made it look as much like Xmas as possible. We had a very nice concert. We were honoured by the presence of a Mayor, a Mayoress and their daughter, who gave us a song. Several of the officers rendered help in the way of songs, and the NCOs and men completed an altogether enjoyable evening. We always continue to make the outlook seem brighter somehow or other. The weather out here is rough – first it's rain, then it's frost, then snow, then it will thaw and freeze again. You will have an idea now what it's like. Of course, I forgot to mention the mud. That is one of the biggest items I think. Apart from the unpleasantness which arises from the abovementioned discomforts, I must say we fare pretty well. We have almost everything necessary under the circumstances, so we must not grumble, because there is many a poor fellow worse off than what we are.

Another letter came from a cavalry boy in France.

It has been a strange Christmas for us, being so far away from home; but when duty calls we must be ready to respond and to sacrifice all. I am here to do my best, and by God's help I will do it. We want no half-hearted men over here; we want whole-hearted men – men who will face the foe willingly. God grant that we may all return home safe, rejoicing with victory. We all got a present from Princess Mary, and a card wishing us a Happy Christmas and a Victorious New Year. We are living under rough conditions, but I am standing it very well, and have got hardened to it. We have a great deal of rain at present and it makes it very damp and cold, but we are well clothed for the purpose. The Indian Soldiers are a fine set of men. Most of them can speak English very well. It opens one's eyes to see the many different sights as we travel along the country. I have not been very near to the firing line yet, but I can hear the roar of the big guns day and night continually. I have not met any of our old boys yet, but I may do so as time goes on. I am enclosing a photo of myself. I would like to have another letter from you whenever you have time to write, as I am always looking and longing for letters from the Dear Old Home.

Another letter was from a boy in the British Expeditionary Force.

Just a line to thank you for the welcome letter. I was very pleased to hear that a lot of the old orphan boys have joined the colours, and I saw by the letter that some have joined the Navy. I hope all the boys and girls in the Orphanage will have a happy time of it this Christmas and New Year as I did when I was in the Home. I often think I would like to see the little cot that I used to have when I was in the Orphan Home at Wilpshire. I was working in Barrow shipyard when the war broke out, and I straightaway went to enlist and was accepted; so when I come back again I will come to see you all to tell you about the glorious victory we will then have had over the Germans.

A boy who had not enlisted but was now a clerk in London described the wartime city.

I don't think you would recognise London if you were to come here now. Everything is in semi-darkness. All the talk is about the Great War. Across the way from where I stay there are about 200 soldiers stationed, and every day at the railway station I see at least one train of them go through. The sky is lit up at nights by the search lights, which are to locate the Zeppelins when they arrive. Guns have been placed on the Marble Arch and all the notable buildings.

Tom Kenyon wrote from HM torpedo boat *Destroyer*. He had been admitted to the orphanage in 1901, after both his parents had died and his sister, who had looked after him, had fallen ill with consumption. He spent three years at the orphanage before going out to a variety of jobs, finally joining the navy in 1910.

I suppose a good many people are wondering what the Navy is doing, but I can assure them that some of those people would know alright if they were on the North Sea Patrol on board a Torpedo Boat, the weather we have had. But we are not downhearted yet! I hope you all had a good old Christmas at the Orphanage. We were at sea, and we knew it, too, on Christmas night. We had a nice Christmas present for a German warship in the form of a torpedo, but none came our way. Well, I am pleased to say that since I wrote to you last I passed an examination for a higher rating, and am now a Leading Stoker, and will shortly go through for Stoker Petty Officer. Kindly give all at the Orphanage and Mrs and The Misses Dixon my best wishes for the New Year, and I know that all the Old Boys who are on active service will, thanks to the splendid training received at the Blackburn Orphanage, do our little bit willingly to silence Germany for ever.

Tom survived the war, and was promoted to leading stoker and much later, in 1928, let James Dixon know he was now serving as chief petty officer, on HMS *Dragon*.

In the orphanage, the girls were doing their bit to support the soldiers and sailors serving their country by knitting socks and scarves. The wool for this venture was donated by various orphanage friends, and parcels of finished work were regularly sent to Lady French, who organised their distribution amongst the troops. By the end of 1915 the tally of finished articles was a hundred and twelve pairs of stockings and socks, twelve scarves and ten pairs of mittens.

During 1915, the orphanage saw no serious diseases, which was a blessing, especially as common diseases such as measles had been rife in the area. However, the costs of running the orphanage had increased dramatically. The war had caused an immediate increase in the prices of food and all the other necessities, and after just one year of war the orphanage was costing a staggering forty per cent more to run. The call on the kindness and generosity of regular friends and subscribers was now more urgent than ever.

In addition, the number of applications for admission to the orphanage was swollen by requests from children who had lost their fathers in the war. Requests also regularly came from servicemen who were already widowers and who had no one else to care for their children, who were therefore effectively homeless. In support of these brave men, the committee had a policy of unrestricted access for such children, but the numbers were problematical.

The list of 'old boys' who had joined the Forces had also risen; over fifty were now fighting for King and Country. One of them came to visit, home for the first time after twelve months spent at the Front in France and gave £2 to the orphanage *'bread and butter'* fund.

Jeremiah Cain had been wounded and wrote home from Rouen Military Hospital.

I was very pleased to receive your welcome letter. I am getting on all right again now, and I think I will be out in a day or two. I am very glad to hear that John Joe Casson is in the Army, and has been out here now fourteen months. I have been out thirteen months, but have had no luck to get leave yet. I am very sorry about Willie Moss being wounded, and wish good luck to all the boys that have joined the colours. I hope all in the Home are in the best of health, and I hope, with a bit of luck, to come and see you all some day.

Jeremiah had come to the orphanage in 1906, when he was ten. His mother had been promised marriage but was deserted and as she needed to continue working, Jeremiah was cared for by his grandmother. When both her husband and her son died and left her penniless, grandmother was obliged to leave her home and go into lodgings with friends, leaving Jeremiah without a home also. Grandmother did not lose touch with her grandson, and as soon as he was of working age, in 1910, he went to live with her again. Like so many of James's children, he kept in touch with his friends at the orphanage and informed James with pride when he joined the Army in

September 1914, very soon after war had been declared. He was just eighteen, and he was immediately sent to France. As his letter says, he was wounded within a year and once recovered, was sent home. He came to visit in July 1916, and said he was now living again with his grandmother in Cumberland. The severity of his wounds is not known, but we do know they were serious enough for him to be discharged instead of being sent back to the Front.

John Joe Casson, mentioned in Jeremiah's letter, was a couple of years older than Jeremiah but close enough for them to know each other well when the orphanage was home to them both. John's mother had died and sadly his stepmother treated him and his two younger brothers very badly. Like Jeremiah, he enlisted in September 1914 and was immediately sent to France.

At Christmas-time 1915, John Joe Casson sent his own letter to James Dixon. This was the second Christmas he had spent in France, and he wrote that he hoped very much to spend the next one at the orphanage.

The horrors of this dreadful War still hang upon us with no end in sight as yet. I often recall the happy days I spent in the Orphanage at Wilpshire. I can imagine the excitement of all the boys and girls at this festive season, and all their hearts filled with joy. I wish I could share their joy. Many a time I wish I had my little cot out here that I used to sleep in when at the Orphanage, instead of having to sleep on hard boxes of ammunition, as I have to do here. Of course, I have got used to it now. I cannot express how thankful I am to you for your great and thoughtful kindness to me in sending a parcel, which arrived safely this afternoon. I am very thankful for the Magazine. I like to read about the old Home, it helps to cheer me up. I am sure there is not one of the 'Old Boys' out here but what his thoughts will go right back to the old Home at Wilpshire, especially on Christmas Day. I must now close with best wishes for a speedy victory for the Allies. Your affectionate scholar, John Joe Casson.

John Casson survived the war relatively unscathed, and was for many years a chauffeur. Like Jeremiah, he kept in touch with his old home for many years.

Another old boy, Thomas Bell, wrote home from Aldershot, having enlisted almost three months before, in July 1915.

When I recall the times I had in the Orphanage, I find things are very hard in the outside world. Oh, that those days could come again; but we have a hard task in front of us to fight the Germans. I have slept eleven weeks under canvas – no boards, only an oil-sheet and a couple of blankets. This all happens in forming a new Battalion and getting us ready for foreign service. Up at 5-30, and often called to night parades, which are very tiresome. But, as you often told us, a soldier must always be prepared to do his duty. There is no finer thing for a man than military life.

Thomas Bell had come to the orphanage as a six-year-old, with his twin brother John. His mother had died giving birth to the twins, and his father had struggled for six years to bring them up, along with his four other children. Finally, very much in debt, in very low spirits, he saw no choice but to seek help. Thomas and his brother had lived at the orphanage until they were fourteen and able to work.

Thomas was eventually sent to France, but none of the preparation he had endured at Aldershot was enough to prevent him being badly wounded and taken prisoner by the Germans. He was eventually released in 1918, some months before the war ended, and was discharged because of his wounds. He called at his old home in May, and James noted in his Occurrences Book that Thomas had been *'shot through the head and lost his eye.'*

Compared to these letters, from young men thrust into adulthood through the rigours of warfare, the following letter from a boy who had recently been sent out to a job bears all the innocence of childhood.

I am trying to do my work well, and I get plenty of good food. I have not got paid yet, but when I get my first wages I will send something towards the orphans' Christmas Pudding Fund. I am going to be honest, and obey those who are over me. I will say my prayers morning and night. I shall be true to my pledge against smoking and drinking. We have three cows, two young calves, two horses and a trap, some greenhouses, an orchard, and two pigs. I send my best love to all at the Blackburn Orphanage.

1916 was a milestone for the orphanage and more particularly for James and Jane Dixon, who would be celebrating two events: James Dixon's 60th birthday, and their Silver Wedding. James's birthday was actually in December 1915, and it was duly celebrated privately with a birthday party for the benefit of the orphanage children, but the committee decided to have a more public dual celebration the following March on the occasion of the couple's wedding anniversary. The event would be marked with the purchase of twin portraits, large framed photographs, which would be paid for by subscriptions. These subscriptions were limited to one shilling per person, a small amount but one designed to allow as many people as possible to be included in the gift. It was expected that hundreds would like to contribute, and this expectation was not misguided.

On Thursday March 16th 1916, James Dixon and his wife Jane were formally presented with the portraits, which had been prepared and framed in dark oak by their friend, Mr Airey. As always, the proceedings commenced with a hymn, a prayer, and a scripture reading. William Tattersall, chairman of the committee, then gave an address, pointing out that this was the first time in thirty years that any real recognition had been made of the work the Dixons had achieved.

We are not met here to flatter, but in a small way to honour our friends in their work of labour and love. To flatter would be out of place, and distasteful, but warmly to appreciate excellent service is the right thing to do. The two Orphanage Buildings and the large school in Bent Street are the result of following a gleam, a thought – the out-going of love and sympathy for poor lost boys and girls.

James Dixon and John Walkden, then two obscure and unknown men, moved by the sad condition of poor children in the streets, were led to attempt something to help them. The start was neither ambitious nor of great promise. First in Leyland Street – a very poor locality; but it proved to be in the right quarter – only a hundred yards from the present School. Then the old School in Bent Street was secured. Very soon houses were taken in Paradise Terrace, Fielden Street and Barley Lane, where began the work of finding lodgings and homes for homeless boys and girls. This was both difficult and expensive. It was then that the thought arose in Mr Dixon's mind: Why not have a Home of our own! That was the germ from which have grown these Orphanage buildings, like the small seed which grew to be a large tree, and the birds lodged in its branches, so this small beginning has provided a home - a real home - for hundreds of poor children. Well may we say, 'What hath God wrought' by those moved with compassion and seeking Divine guidance in work which is His work? Mr Dixon would not claim these results as his, but we will say that probably this Orphanage would not have been here but for him.

I have often said I would rather be Mr Dixon, with his work, than the most successful business man or millionaire with nothing to show but money. Mr Dixon's life has been a noble success. Of course, the help of thousands have been brought in. Sympathy, naturally, turns to the orphan, but the work done here has largely developed that sympathy, because confidence has been inspired in the management; and this chiefly in the character of Mr and Mrs Dixon at its head.

Mr Dixon has been most successful in raising funds for this work. First, by his own gifts; then by untiring labour. I am sorry we have not here today Mr Thomas Hart to undertake the pleasant duty that has fallen upon me. Mr Hart, along with Mr Dixon, joined in the first hundred pounds given towards this Orphanage, each contributing fifty pounds. Mr Hart is still a strong supporter. We are sorry a bad cold prevents him from being present today.

The work at the Ragged School, Bent Street, has grown beyond all expectations, 800 to 1,000 children and young persons being present *every Sunday. Besides this, there are many forms of Christian activity. The lower room is all alive on winter evenings with youths enjoying all kinds of recreation who might otherwise be in the streets.*

The Cripple Committee is in touch with about 200 cripples all the year round. There is also the Cripples' Home, at Livesey. Another branch of work is the distribution of second-hand clothing, shoes, and clogs to poor cases, and visitation of the sick. The School is a beehive of religious and philanthropic work under the devoted management of Mr Chilman and a large number of voluntary workers.

These photographs are the spontaneous expression of affection and admiration from a wide circle of friends. Hundreds of subscribers have sent their shillings (and many were ready to give more) and have expressed their personal appreciation of Mr and Mrs Dixon's work. We might say these buildings are a monument to Mr and Mrs Dixon, but the richest memorial of our friends is in the hearts of hundreds of men and women – once children here – now scattered all over the world.

These portraits will hang upon the Walls of this Orphanage, and, as their inscriptions read, will be a permanent expression of the love and work to which Mr and Mrs Dixon have given their lives.

The portraits were then unveiled by two of the youngest children currently in the orphanage and James Dixon then gave a speech on behalf of himself and his wife.

Mr Chairman, Ladies and Gentlemen; Thirty-six years ago, in Blackburn I accidentally found about half-a-dozen little boys sleeping out. They were crouched in the doorway of a warehouse. Soon after, other homeless boys and girls came under my notice and were helped in every way I could. About that time I had a dream – but it was then only a dream – to establish an Orphanage for homeless boys and girls. The dream has now been realised, and the present handsome pile of buildings is the outcome of 36 years' hard work.

I remember going into the common lodging-houses late one night to see if any little child needed help, and crossing King William Street, I saw a poor boy warming his hands at a red fire on the street, just under the Market Clock, where the stone sets had been removed for repairs. Placing my hand on his shoulder, I said: 'What are you doing here, my boy; why don't you go home to your father and mother? Look at the clock, it's just going to strike 12 midnight, all little boys should be in bed!'

'I have no father or mother and no home', said the boy.

'Where did you sleep last night?' I said.

'In a lodging house,' was the reply.

'Then why don't you go there tonight,' I asked.

'Because I have no money, and they won't let me in unless I pay 3d a night,' was the answer.

I took the boy into the Home, where he had a good supper, a warm bath, and was soon fast asleep among the blankets. The boy's story proved to be true. He stayed with us about six years, and is now usefully employed in a situation, doing well, a good citizen, and a sincere Christian lad. This is typical of many other cases the Institute has helped to rescue and to save.

This being our Silver Wedding, I am glad that my dear wife and partner in life has been so kindly remembered by presenting her also with her portrait, today. In my youth I was blessed with a Godly father and a praying mother, and for 25 years have had a good wife and a real helpmeet, who is in complete sympathy with me in the work among poor children.

In all the masses of documents in the orphanage archives, there is little mention of Jane, so it is pleasing to see her mentioned on such a momentous occasion. It should not be forgotten that it was Jane, as matron, who had the bulk of the daily responsibility of caring for more than a hundred children, making sure they were fed, clothed, educated and nursed through their illnesses. Her work may have been done quietly and without remark, but it was just as valuable as the work her husband did in raising the money to allow their mission to children to continue.

Elsie Muriel, James's daughter, had now completed her education and joined her mother and father in their work, becoming assistant matron in 1915. As part of her duties she took on the task of writing the regular column *For The Young* in the monthly editions of *Rags and Rubies.* In her column she told her young readers how many old boys and girls had been in touch regarding her parents' Silver Wedding and her father's birthday, and quoted from some of the letters they had received from all over the world.

In the same magazine which reported James's sixtieth birthday, it was also noted that the orphanage's *Roll of Honour*, listing those old boys who had enlisted for service in the war, had now risen to sixty-three. Another old boy had lost his life. Joseph Marsden came to the orphanage as a nine-year-old in 1903 along with his brother Henry. Their father had died from pneumonia four years previously and their mother was working full-time in service but not earning enough to support her children. Joseph stayed in the orphanage until he was old enough to work and then worked as a farm labourer for seven years, eventually joining the navy. By 1915 he was on the HMS *Invincible*, a battle cruiser. During the Battle of Jutland, in May 1916, the Invincible was the flagship of her squadron, until she was hit by the German navy on May 31st. She sank in the North Sea near the Orkney Islands, and Joseph was drowned.

Six other 'old boys' were so far known to be wounded:

Sergeant Aspin, who was wounded in France, on the 20th July last, is now in Ellerslie Hospital, Blackburn. He has wounds on the head, hand, and right arm; a bullet has also been extracted from his breast. He was wounded in the big fight during the British 'push,' in July. From the field hospital, near the trenches, he was removed to the Base Hospital, and on by easy stages to England. Arriving at Southampton, he was taken to Fallowfield Military Hospital, Manchester, and then afterwards transferred to Ellerslie, Blackburn, where he is now making a good recovery, and speaks highly of the kind treatment he receives there.

In October 1916, with the war now two years old, Elsie Muriel wrote very intelligently on the subject to her young readers.

The weary War still continues its cruel course, entailing untold misery and suffering to thousands of homes from which millions of brave boys have gone to face perils on land and sea; many to make the supreme sacrifice. The tide of war has now turned in our favour, and our forces are adding victory to victory. But there is much to do yet, and we cannot afford to rest on our oars. We are not fighting for territory or for self-aggrandisement, but for ideals, for honour, and for the rights of small nations, and so we pray God to prosper our righteous cause, and give us the victory in His own good time and way.

Elsie Muriel went on to describe gifts which had recently arrived at the orphanage, including one donation from a local family, in memory of their son who had been killed in June 1915. Then she talked about another donation from her own uncle and aunt, who had lost their only son, her cousin Harold, in July 1916. He was just nineteen years old. She quoted from a newspaper article about him.

Lieutenant McLellan was an engineering pupil when the War began. He enlisted in the first month of the War, on his 18th birthday, as a private, and was given his first commission from a Manchester Battalion in March, 1915, and passing through the special reserve for officers was commissioned in his own line regiment in February this year. He had almost completed twelve months service in France. His colonel writes: 'I am very sorry to lose him, as he was an excellent officer, and showed great courage, and he was much liked by his brother officers. He was doing very good work when hit.'

Elsie Muriel was aware that many of her young readers – and the older ones too – were similarly affected by loss in their own families, and this account of her cousin's death showed solidarity with her readers.

While I mourn the loss of my cousin Harold I am not unmindful of many more who are in deep sorrow because of the untimely end of their near and dear ones, killed in their youth at the 'Front' on the battlefield, or who have been drowned in the sea fights on the mighty deep. Your sincere friend, Elsie Muriel.

There was also one very sad death to report at the orphanage. The Annual Report for 1916 reported the death of Thurston Moorcroft. Aged fourteen, he had been a resident for five years, along with his four brothers and sisters. He had only been ill for a couple of days and his illness was not thought severe enough to call a doctor urgently. His was only the fifth death to occur in the orphanage in twenty-five years – three of whom were buried in Salesbury churchyard and the fourth in the public cemetery on his relatives' request. Thurston's funeral began with a short service at the orphanage, before the procession to the church where older boys from the orphanage carried the coffin to the graveside.

By 1916, the orphanage's Roll of Honour listed sixty-eight old boys now in the forces engaged in the war. Five had now lost their lives. Elsie Muriel's monthly letter *For The Young* included a poem sent by Percy Conway, who was then on a minesweeper vessel; he had sent the poem with a silk bookmark for Christmas.

I'm knocking about on the briny sea,
Where the British Fleet is sailing,
Sweeping the mines which are always near,
And friends, and the other chaps, hailing;
It isn't exactly a 'pleasure trip,'
Carrying on in cold and storm,
But at least the work in this old ship
Is enough to keep a youth warm.
Now I'm sending this line that soon you'll get,
With the hope that this Sailor you'll not forget,
Who, though on the Ocean, is all serene.
From Percy Conway (Signalman).
H.M.S. Godetia (Fleet Mine Sweeper).

By 1917 there were over a hundred old boys in the Forces, the death toll of old boys killed at war had risen to seven and the girls in the orphanage had knitted two hundred and twenty-two articles for their part in the War Effort. The costs of running the orphanage had doubled, and from other parts of the country, news was beginning to come to James of several homes which had been forced to close entirely because of the rapidly rising costs of keeping them open. Wilpshire orphanage managed to survive only because of the vigorous efforts of friends, supporters, and the local population but even then, essential repairs and repainting jobs had to be postponed.

In October 1917, one terrifying night, it seemed that the war had come closer to home, when everyone in the orphanage was woken by the unnerving noise of explosions. They were some way off in the distance, but powerful enough so that the windows in the building shuddered with the force. This was the first time the sounds of warfare had invaded the normally peaceful environment, and the only possible explanation seemed to be that German Zeppelins were bombing the area.

James Dixon and the other orphanage staff told all the children to dress and herded them down into the basement areas of both buildings, where they distracted themselves by singing songs and hymns whilst the explosions continued for more than three hours. The children were put back to bed (without undressing) sometime after two in the morning, where they slept soundly till breakfast time.

The following evening, all was explained when a police sergeant visited the orphanage with the news that Lancaster Munitions Works had suffered a devastating fire, started by accident, and which had caused the endless explosions as it spread mercilessly through the large complex of buildings, detonating shells as it progressed.

As the war dragged on the letters quoted in Elsie Muriel's columns began to illustrate emotions quite different from those expressed in 1914, when everyone was hopeful that the war would last only a matter of months before victory was won. In July 1918, one old boy wrote '… *a few hasty lines to let you know that I am a prisoner of war in Germany, being wounded and captured near Cambrai. I have lost my right eye and my hearing is almost gone. I trust the war won't last much longer. I am longing to see you all again. It is two years since I left dear old Lancashire. Please remember me to all at the orphanage, and give my best respects to the officers and all the boys and girls.'*

Another wrote from France, saying '*The war cloud is still black and dark, but there is a better time in store and we must press on to victory.*'

It was also in that month that the whole country was ravaged by influenza, an illness which at that time was debilitating, and which could result in life-threatening conditions and even death. James Dixon's Occurrences Book records the number of cases amongst the orphanage children, a number which rose every day.

July 28 Dr Aitchison called at the Orphanage today to see 14 of the boys down with Influenza.

July 29 Dr Aitchison called today, all the boys are much better.

July 30 Dr Aitchison called at the Orphanage today, we now have 25 children down with Influenza.

July 31 Dr Aitchison called at the Orphanage today & saw the sick children who are all improving.

Aug 1 Thirty-six children are now down with Influenza. All are doing fairly well.

Aug 2 Forty-nine children now with Influenza.

Aug 3 Dr W R Pollard called at the Orphanage today.

Aug 4 Dr W R Pollard called today, all the children improving.

Aug 5 We have now sixty children down with Influenza.

Aug 6 Several of the children have now recovered and out of bed.

136

Aug 7   Dr W R Pollard called. All the children are improving.

Aug 8   The total number of children in the Orphanage who have been attacked with Influenza is 63. (32 boys & 31 girls.)

Only one child lost his battle against this virulent disease: Fred Butcher, whose heart was weak. He had little natural defence, and the influenza quickly progressed to pneumonia. His funeral took place on August 1st and took the habitual form of a service at the orphanage before the procession to Salesbury Church, where the little boy was laid to rest in the orphanage grave. A memorial service was held for him on the following Sunday.

The Annual Report and orphanage magazines during 1918 were, once again, full of news and reports from the war, now in its fourth awful year. In April, there was another threat, more real this time, that the war was about to come to Blackburn, when the police came at midnight to warn James Dixon that a German air raid might well occur. All the officers were woken so that they would be ready to rouse the children and move them to the basements if the bombing started, and everyone stayed awake and ready until four in the morning - when a message came by telephone that, thankfully, the danger had not materialised.

In the summer, the orphanage played host to a number of wounded soldiers from Queen's Park Military Hospital, who were entertained in the sunny orphanage field. The girls sang for the soldiers, games were played, refreshments were served and the soldiers returned back to the hospital cheered by a happy afternoon.

And finally, on the 11th of November, peace was declared – an occasion which some must have thought would never arrive. James Dixon recorded the event in his diary prosaically, *'1918 Nov 11 'Peace Day' end of the great war. Went to dentist.'*

At the orphanage, this news was received with joy; as church bells pealed out from all directions, the building was decked with streamers and the flagstaff was adorned with both the Union Jack and the Stars and Stripes. James wrote about the celebrations in the orphanage magazine, describing how the children ran home from school singing patriotic songs to find a party awaiting them with sweets and fireworks, followed by a more sober Thanksgiving service in the orphanage schoolroom. James quoted from one of the hymns he had chosen for the occasion.

God bless our soldiers, Guard them each day,
Make them victorious, O'er all the way:
In the great conflict, may they endure;
God bless our soldiers, Make victory sure.

James Dixon ended his piece in the magazine by reflecting on the fact that after the celebrations were over, the aftermath of the war had hardly started.

And, oh! to think of it still going on, and alas! Thousands of bereaved and saddened hearts and homes. And sometimes I ponder and think: Are we as a nation any nearer God, and better and nobler living than we were then? There is still the selfishness, greed and lust; and the hateful Drink still holds sway, apparently unheeded and unchallenged by many professing Christians. God grant that after all this sacrifice of blood, tears, and agony, there may yet rise a nobler and better race, and that England may yet be the first modern nation to put Jesus Christ upon the throne and acknowledge and proclaim Him king and ruler over all.

James would never forget that a hundred and sixteen of his boys had enlisted in the Army or Navy and entered the horrors of trench warfare, where many had been injured both in body and mind. By the time Peace Day was celebrated, the number of his brave boys who had lost their lives had risen to ten:

Jacob Aspin.
Alfred Burns.
William Cowell.
John Thomas Crook.

Thomas Hutton.
John Hutton.
Joseph Marsden.
William North.
William Siddorn.
William Wilcock.

Jacob Aspin, John Thomas Crook and Alfred Burns had been amongst the first children admitted to the orphanage in 1891.

Joseph Marsden, as already noted, drowned when his ship, The Invincible, went down in the North Sea in May 1916.

William Wilcock had come to the orphanage aged eleven in 1899, after his father died and his mother deserted him and his two younger sisters. When he was of age he had gone to work as a draper's assistant. He enlisted in the army in 1915, and died in France in May 1917.

William Cowell, eight, came to the orphanage in 1903 after his father died leaving his mother struggling to support four small children – he went back to live with his mother as soon as he was old enough to work. He enlisted in December 1915 and with his regiment went to Mesopotamia, where he died in action in April 1917.

Thomas and John Hutton, brothers, came to the orphanage in 1900, aged nine and seven after their father died leaving their mother in poverty. Thomas went home to his mother when he was old enough to work; John went to work as a farm boy. Both boys joined the Army at the outbreak of war, and both died in 1916, Thomas in August and John in October.

William Siddorn had come as a ten-year-old to the orphanage in 1909, after both his parents died of tuberculosis. When he was of age, he first worked as a farmer's boy, but by 1916 he was living in Barrow and working in the munition works there, as yet too young to enlist. By July 1917, a month after his eighteenth birthday, he had enlisted and he wrote to James Dixon from Aldershot where he was training. Nine months later he died, at Flanders in France.

The last of the ten 'old boys' who lost their lives in the World War was William North; fatherless and from a pauper family, he had come to the orphanage as a nine-year-old in 1902. Poignantly, the archives give us no further detail about his death, but like the rest, he would never be forgotten.

In November 1919, at the eleventh hour of the eleventh day, the flag was lowered to half-mast and at the King's request, everyone at the orphanage gathered to observe a two minute silence. Before the silence, James Dixon read out the names of the ten old boys who had fallen in the war. It was the beginning of a new tradition, which would be observed for many years to come.

CHAPTER THIRTEEN

Two months after the war ended, in January 1919, James's second daughter Elsie Muriel married. Her husband was Arthur Clifford Booth (Cliff), a Naval man. Their first child, a boy, was born two years later, in February 1921. Three weeks later, in what was arguably the greatest tragedy of James Dixon's life, Elsie Muriel died. There is a brief mention of this event in the orphanage's Occurrences Book, noted in accordance with routine, because Elsie was, after all, a member of staff. The entry was simple, factual and to the point, James's hand-writing tremulous with grief. It was not the first death the orphanage had witnessed, nor would it be the last, but one cannot help but feel for James, as he recorded this terrible event as a matter of duty.

A little later, James wrote about his loss more fully, in the process of compiling the next edition of the orphanage magazine. He needed to explain to the young readers of Elsie's regular column that they would no longer be hearing from her.

Dear young friends,

For many years this column with the usual 'Letter To The Young' has appeared over the signature 'Elsie Muriel', my married daughter – Mrs A.C. Booth – better known by her maiden name of Elsie Muriel Dixon.

It is now my painful duty to announce with very very deep regret her sudden death, which occurred on March 9th last. The public announcement of our sad bereavement appeared in The Weekly Telegraph as follows:-

'The death took place on Wednesday of Mrs A.C. Booth, of Wilpshire, second daughter of Mr and Mrs J Dixon, of Blackburn Orphanage. Mrs Booth was married two years ago to Mr A.C. Booth, FRA, who holds an appointment as engineer on HMS Thunderer. Her death, in her twenty-fifth year, has been a severe shock to her relatives, and means a loss to

the activities of the Wilpshire Orphanage, for in many ways she has associated herself with the interests of the Institution. Her contribution to the Magazine was always a source of great pleasure to the young folks, and in other ways she had the children's well-being at heart. By means of the organised sale of scent packets she has raised over £140 towards the Orphanage funds.

'The funeral took place on Saturday, March 12th, 1921, at Salesbury Churchyard. The Rev T.W. Walker, MA, Vicar, officiated at the graveside.'

Elsie Muriel was a great help to her mother and I in the work among orphan and destitute children at the orphanage during the past 12 years. Her influence for good among the children was most remarkable. Her loving, kindly disposition, linked to a character of singular sweetness and sincerity, made her a beloved figure among the orphan boys and girls to whom she gave the best of her young life of untiring devotion. Among the many wreaths laid on her grave was one from the orphanage children, who will miss her very much as indeed we all do.

Elsie's baby son was baptised at the orphanage the day after his mother's funeral. He was christened John Dixon Booth. He stayed at the orphanage in James's and Jane's care, but this was not an ideal situation for his father Cliff, who could seldom see him. Consequently, when he was seven months old, he went to live with Cliff's uncle in Rotherham, and was brought up by Cliff's family from then on. James and Jane made regular visits and little John came to stay with them also, from time to time, but one can guess that for a couple so devoted to children, the separation from their tiny motherless grandson must have been painful.

James Dixon was fortunate to have good health throughout his life; indeed only one spell of illness is recorded, in September of 1922, which was noted by the Weekly Telegraph as an unusual event.

Having recovered from a brief but prostrating spell of illness, Mr James Dixon, the veteran head of the Wilpshire Orphanage, is now out and

142

about again, and as hard at work as ever. The experience had been a new one for him, and it has brought to light one fact testifying to that physical hardihood on which he has every reason to pride himself, the fact that until a month ago he had passed through fifty years without the attention of a doctor. And on the first Sunday that he was allowed out of doors he went off to Grindleton, conducted three services, paid numerous calls in the interests of the Orphanage, and walked seven or eight miles into the bargain.

Jane Dixon's health had also been good, but in the summer of 1926 she fell ill and, as her illness progressed, a nurse was engaged for her. It was most likely her illness which brought James to the decision to finally move from the orphanage, which had been the couple's life-long home, to a smaller house in Walden Road which, in a nostalgic moment and in memory of James's family roots, they christened Annandale. The house was actually bought by their daughter Gertrude, who married Henry Whittaker a year later and went to live with him in their own house in Great Harwood. Six months later, in March 1928, James's life-long wife, partner and helpmeet, Jane, passed away.

James may have been in good health, but when Jane died he was seventy-three years old, and whilst he would remain involved with the orphanage in the highest degree until the end of his life, without Jane he could not continue in the same way. His daughter Gertrude was married, his daughter Isabella had qualified as a teacher and would soon move to Surrey and so it was time to look outside the family for successors to his role. The chosen couple were Mr and Mrs Tom Street, whose names are as familiar to those who know the orphanage as James and Jane Dixon's own names. It was a good choice. The Streets were appointed as assistant superintendent and matron in 1928, and would remain in office for over thirty years.

James continued his work in whatever way he could; during 1929 the Annual Report noted that he had given addresses in local churches and chapels on ninety-five occasions, and had encouraged over a hundred Sunday School collections. He also gave the Endowment Fund £500, in memory of Jane. Her cot's plaque bore the inscription *'The Jane Dixon (Mother) Cot 1929'.*

It is not easy to think of James living alone in *Annandale* after spending the majority of his life surrounded by family, colleagues and, most of all, children. It was not a situation which lasted long, however, for in 1931, James's daughter Gertrude and her husband came to live with him permanently and in the spring of 1933 gave him the great joy of a granddaughter, christened Nancy Muriel. Two years later, in December 1935, James celebrated the great milestone of his eightieth birthday. The Blackburn Times carried a lengthy article about the celebrations.

Wednesday was a landmark in the history of the Blackburn Orphanage, and a day that will long be remembered by the children, for it marked the 80th birthday of the founder and superintendent, Mr. James Dixon, an occasion which was celebrated with all due ceremony. This unique occasion was recognised by a presentation to Mr. Dixon, who, after nearly half a century's service at the Orphanage, is still doing tremendously good work and is as active as ever.

Presiding over the presentation, Mr. J. Pearson (chairman of the Trust Committee) spoke of the vitality of Mr. Dixon, who, he said, not only roamed about Blackburn every day, picking up money and ideas for the Orphanage, but preached two and sometimes three sermons every Sunday. He likened the Orphanage to a junior Dr Barnardo's Home.

The presentation consisted of an electric clock from the children and staff, with the following inscription: 'To Father Dixon, on his 80th birthday, December 11th, 1935 from the children and staff of Blackburn Orphanage, as a token of great love and affection', and from the committee a wireless set, bearing the inscription: 'To Mr James Dixon, on the occasion of his 80th birthday. From the Orphanage Committee, as a token of affection and esteem, December 11th, 1935.'

On behalf of the children, Fred Wilson, a 9-year-old inmate, said: 'We orphans are perhaps the only ones who can appreciate the benefactions bestowed upon us by Mr. Dixon's wonderful idea forty eight years ago to build a home for such children as us.' Therefore they thought on the occasion of his 80th birthday they should show their appreciation. The clock was handed over by Mary Robinson, a 9-year-old girl.

In reply, Mr. Dixon told the story of how the Orphanage was founded. In 1886, he said, he had a dream to found the Orphanage. He put £50 into the bank that year towards the building fund, and the late Mr. Thomas Hart, J.P., put in a similar amount. As a result the first building was opened in 1891. His whole dream had not yet been fulfilled, but much had been done and the Orphanage had done a noble and wonderful work.

Mr Dixon said he had received messages of goodwill from all parts of the country, and even further afield. Amongst them was one from an old girl of the Orphanage, who sent 10 shillings and grateful thanks; and one from one of the first boys he had helped 45 years ago, who was now doing well in Australia. He had sent a lamb to Australia House, London, to be forwarded to the Orphanage for Christmas Day. There was also a message from an old boy who had become a police inspector.

Christmas came only three weeks after this great celebration, but was as enjoyable as any the orphanage had seen. Decorations filled the corridors and the dining rooms, and both the boys' and girls' buildings had their own tree, laden with gifts for the children.

On Christmas Eve, after the children had gone to bed, Father Christmas visited in person and went from dormitory to dormitory, waking all the children up again and distributing presents for them to open. But despite their late night, the children would be woken early the next morning, for a busy Christmas Day.

Early on Christmas morning, the older girls sang carols, rousing Matron and Staff, after which they followed the old custom of 'breaking into' the boys' building to wish the lads 'a merry Christmas.' The breakfast tables, decorated with miniature Christmas trees, were filled with sweets, oranges, apples, and handkerchiefs. In the excitement, little or no breakfast was eaten.

Later, Mr Pearson (Chairman), Mr. Dixon {Superintendent), and the children, with members of the Trust Committee and friends, welcomed the Mayor and Mayoress. The youngsters sang carols and listened with interest to the Mayor's Christmas greeting. New pennies were distributed to each of them, through the generosity of Mr W.Y. Gowans, of Whalley; the workpeople of Messrs. Jones Textiles, who provided mistletoe forfeits; and Mr. Sagar Jones Mitchell.

The children afterwards assembled as one large family in an endeavour to dispose of 19 turkeys and 30 plum puddings. During the meal, selections were played by Wilpshire Prize Band. The afternoon was quietly spent in preparation for tea, which consisted of fancies, slab cake, Christmas cakes, jellies, and other good things. The huge trees were illuminated and the Christmas spirit was felt everywhere.

In the evening, nine of the children, led by Mr T. Street, Assistant Superintendent, with Miss Edmund at the piano, gave a concert, thus bringing a tiring, but happy day to a close.

It was James Dixon's last Christmas in the orphanage. He died, aged eighty, on May 17th 1936. There is perhaps no better commentary on his life and his passing than that which was printed in the Blackburn Times, the following week.

THE ORPHANS FRIEND

It was perhaps fitting that Mr. James Dixon, of Walden Road, who died on Sunday evening, May 17th, 1936, should pass away in the Jubilee year of the Blackburn Orphanage which he founded, and which had claimed his constant care since its inception in 1886.

It was Mr. Dixon's great aim to give every child who entered the Orphanage a real chance in life. Those of ability were allowed to sit for scholarships and embark upon professional careers. The strenuousness of the early struggles, the constant vigilance required to maintain the institution, and the care and anxiety of catering for so many deserving cases, called for a degree of thought and energy which only the initiated can understand.

146

Nevertheless, Mr. Dixon never had any regrets, and the hundreds of appreciative letters which he regularly received from old boys and girls who had entered upon useful and often prosperous careers, provided some compensation for all he had tried to do. This veteran Superintendent was not only an administrator of rare ability, but he gave up almost the whole of his leisure lecturing, preaching and speaking of the good work performed at the Home at Wilpshire. In this way he extended the interest and was the means of raising large sums to further the work.

Known to many philanthropists and organisers, Mr Dixon had numerous invitations to leave Wilpshire for more remuneration, but he preferred to carry on with the work to which he had devoted his life. As he approached his 78th birthday he offered to continue as General Secretary without pay, but the committee would not hear of it, and induced him to accept a small pension. He retained his post, however, and was appointed an honorary member of the Committee.

Poignantly, amongst the archives there is a letter dated the day after James died, 18th May 1936, which accompanied an engraved silver tray, presented by Pearson's Fresh Air Fund and the Shaftesbury Society, in honour of James's forty years of involvement with that cause, which raised funds to give poor children holidays in the countryside or by the sea. It was just one more example of James's tireless work for the benefit of poor young people.

James Dixon's funeral, on May 21st, was a relatively quiet affair, his family wishing to keep the event as private as possible, a service being conducted at his home, Annandale, by the Rev. Miller from James's church, St George's. However, many of James's colleagues past and present did attend James's burial at Blackburn Cemetery, along with around fifty boys and girls from the orphanage. Eight of James Dixon's boys bore his coffin to his grave in Blackburn Cemetery: John Edwards, George Clayton, Fred Duckworth, Edward Leaver, William Morris, James Milburn, Harold Hartwell and John Casson, whose history has been previously described in this book. The family also requested no flowers – but four wreaths were nevertheless sent to grace the graveside.

Later that year, the Annual Founder's Day gathering at the orphanage was also the occasion of the unveiling of an oak tablet commemorating James Dixon. The tablet was unveiled by Mrs Yerburgh and the group witnessing the event included trustees and committee members, staff and children, many old boys and girls, and representatives from Salesbury School. Salesbury Church and Wilpshire Methodist Church were also represented. The text on the tablet included these lines: *'His energies were devoted to any duty in which he could serve God and his fellow men.'*

The following year, two beautiful stained glass windows were unveiled at the Ragged School; they were dedicated to the memory of James Dixon and his friend and colleague, John T. Walkden and had been paid for by Mrs Nuttall, JP. The school itself was demolished around the year 2000 and a new one built in its place, but the windows were, happily, preserved and incorporated into the new building.

It is almost unnecessary to add that an orphanage cot was also endowed in James Dixon's name. Like the thirty-seven other endowed beds in the orphanage, it bore a brass plaque and was christened *'The Founder's Cot'.*

The brass plaque and the oak tablet both still survive and are on display in the surviving Wilpshire orphanage building. They stand in memory of this remarkable man, who as a young man made the emotional decision to devote *'the whole of his time'* to helping the most vulnerable of Blackburn's poor and destitute: those who, because of their youth, were wholly undeserving of their plight. James Dixon's intervention in their lives allowed them to fulfil their potential and grow up to lead useful, patriotic and Christian lives.

Appendix

ENDOWED COTS

The money received for this purpose was invested, the annual interest on each amount being enough to support a child for a year. James Dixon's own bequest brought the number of endowed cots to 38 and the following list was printed in the Annual Report for 1936.

1	The Mrs John Pickup Cot	1891
2	The Mrs Frederick Pickup Cot	1891
3	The Daniel Thwaites Cot	1892
4	The Miss Derbyshire Cot	1897
5	The Mrs Sames Cot	1897
6	The Mrs Clayton (Larkhill) Cot	1898
7	The Ann Hoyle Cot	1900
8	The James Hoyle Cot	1900
9	The Ellen Duxbury Cot	1905
10	The Aspinall Clayton Cot	1905
11	The James Bradley Cot	1906
12	The Susannah Bradley Cot	1906
13	The James Wilcock Cot (No 1)	1906
14	The Dorothy Margaret Cot	1908
15	The George Riley Cot	1908
16	The Children's Cot, endowed by the Children of Blackburn and East Lancashire	1909
17	The James Wilcock Cot (No 2)	1911
18	Ditto (No 3)	1912
19	Ditto (No 4)	1912
20	Ditto (No 5)	1912
21	Ditto (No 6)	1912
22	The Maria Mercer Cot (No 1)	1914
23	Ditto (No 2)	1914
24	The Elizabeth Fielding Cot	1916
25	The Nellie Fielding Cot	1916
26	The Arthur Clegg Bowdler Cot	1919

27	The Ann Eliza Bowdler Cot	1919
28	The Mary Ann Smith Cot	1921
29	The Daniel and Mary Sumner Cot	1923
30	The James Blacklock Cot	1923
31	The Milton Haydock Cot	1926
32	The Jane Dixon (Mother) Cot	1929
33	The Mrs Emma Pickop Cot	1929
34	The John Holden Cot	1933
35	The Sir John Rutherford Cot	1933
36	The Margaret and Janet Beattie Cot	1935
37	The I and R E Cotton Cot	1938
38	The Founder's Cot – Mr James Dixon	1938